Jump In:

Women Investing in Women, Growing Our Capital and Impact

Kristina Montague

Foreword by Heather Cabot,
Author of *Geek Girl Rising*

"Money is a form of power. As our wealth grows, women have the opportunity to use their investments to direct where money – and power – flows. Investing in start-up companies led by female CEOs changes the game. Written by an experienced VC, *Jump In* shows you how to join other women who are putting their money to work for a better world."

—JANINE FIRPO,
Author, *Activate Your Money,*
and Co-Founder, Invest for Better

"*Jump In* is filled with story after story of ordinary people doing extraordinary things to help female founders get more access to the capital needed to create real change."

—MARCIA DAWOOD,
Host, *The Angel Next Door* podcast
and Author, *Do Good While Doing Well*

"This book could not have come at a better time. We need to do more than just move the needle. Kristina's story and vision will inspire, educate, and empower the next generation of female investors and entrepreneurs. Innovation and creativity are paramount in creating a sustainable entrepreneurial ecosystem that reflects our values. Reading this book is an important first step in making this happen."

—ALICIA ROBB,
Founder, The Rising Tide and Next Wave Impact Funds;
Author, *The Next Wave: Financing Women's Growth-Oriented Firms*

"This insightful book on investing in women by women provides a compelling case and roadmap for fostering gender diversity in entrepreneurship. Kristina's expertise and nuanced perspective provide an invaluable resource for anyone looking to navigate and reshape the landscape of angel investing and venture capital.

—DAWN BATTS,
Co-Founder, Milestone Growth Capital

"Kristina has a way of diving into the hard topics of investing, economics, community building and leadership development with ease and grace. As a former educator, she leads with education and knowledge to truly empower a movement of more women investors activating their capital. This book is her legacy to the rising tide of investors wanting to do more with their capital—so jump in, enjoy, and be a part of moving historical barriers to change lives and economies."

—DR. SILVIA MAH,
General Partner, Stella Impact Capital;
Author, *The Startup Investor Mindset*

BSB

Published by Big Self Books, an affiliate of Big Self School, LLC
Paperback ISBN: 978-1-945064-16-6
Ebook ISBN: 978-1-945064-17-3
LCCN: Available upon request

Set in Arno Pro with Work Sans
Book design by Catherine Dionne at Goodboy Creative Co.

Printed in the United States of America

To the women who innovate
and those who invest in them.
May we create the change we want
to see in the world, together.

Contents

Foreword

While reporting for *Geek Girl Rising,* my 2017 book with co-author Samantha Walravens, we initially set off in search of the "sisterhood shaking up tech" in all of the typical hot spots. Our research, over more than three years, took us inside startup pitch contests, tech accelerators, engineering conferences, STEM classrooms, and maker spaces across California and New York. We observed high-powered schmoozing at San Francisco's exclusive club, The Battery, where baby-faced founders rubbed elbows with billionaire venture capitalists. We peered inside a sparsely furnished women-only Silicon Valley "Hacker House" in the shadow of Facebook and Google and flew down to Silicon Beach to meet one of the most influential beauty content creators on YouTube. We pounded the pavement for months at a time in Manhattan shadowing ex-Wall Street execs and media veterans investing in scrappy women-led ventures incubated in the eclectic co-working spaces sprouting up in NYC's Silicon Alley. From the Bay Area to Brooklyn, we could have easily centered the entire book on the startup scenes dazzling the news media at the time. But as we met more of the enterprising women helping other women build and fund the businesses of tomorrow, we became increasingly curious about the outliers breathing life into places under the radar, far away from the usual coastal haunts. We wondered, what was happening in the middle of the country?

This is what brought me to Chattanooga, Tennessee on

a muggy afternoon in May of 2016. It was my first-time in Gig City, named for its lightning-fast broadband network luring new industry and jobs to the one-time manufacturing hub along the Tennessee River. I had flown down from New York for a whirlwind trip to better understand how a group of enterprising local women helped to fuel the city's latest renaissance.

As soon as my guide, Kristina Montague met me downtown amid brightly colored murals and renovated warehouses filled with hipster cafes and artisanal shops, I was taken in by the city's energy and by Kristina's infectious enthusiasm. Over the next two days, she introduced me to the inspiring women behind JumpFund, an eclectic collection of small business owners, philanthropists, civic activists, artists, moms, and grandmoms betting tens of thousands of dollars of their own cash on the promise of women-led startups and ventures homegrown in the Southeast. This raucous tribe of whip-smart, outspoken, and serious investors immediately countered the stereotypical image I had conjured in my imagination of delicate Southern belles sipping sweet tea and asking their husbands for permission before writing investment checks. As soon as I got to know a few of the powerhouse partners over a gracious dinner filled with laughs and candid stories, I realized the influence and ambition of this group. The next day, over a series of interviews, several members shared their thoughts on gender lens investing and how they hoped their efforts would alter the economic landscape of their hometown and the region at large. I came home from my visit inspired and with a deep appreciation of their contributions to their community and the impact their story could have on other potential female investors and entrepreneurs across the country.

"Never dim your light for anyone. Shine it on whoever you can shine it on, that's what I love about Chattanooga

women," Cathy Boettner, one of JumpFund's limited partners, explained to me of the mindset that made the group
gel. After spending some time with Cathy and her Jump-
Fund colleagues, I had to agree. They were just as "badass"
as Cathy described to me—and strikingly dedicated to
lifting up one another as well as the burgeoning businesses they infused with startup capital.

As you'll read in Kristina's book, the genesis of Jump-
Fund sparked from the keen observations of a small cohort of Chattanooga women who noticed that the mid-
sized city's fresh efforts to ignite a tech ecosystem weren't
attracting female founders or female investors. The group
raised concerns with local business leaders about the opportunities Chattanooga was missing by ignoring the gender disparity. But their opinions were politely dismissed.
So instead of merely remaining frustrated and sitting on
the sidelines, Kristina and her future partners set out to
prove the naysayers wrong. The story of how they did just
that and went on to collaborate on deals alongside some
of their biggest skeptics is both admirable and empowering and detailed in the following pages, along with a playbook for aspiring angel investors.

Since visiting Chattanooga, I have been thrilled to follow the trajectory of the fund and its partners and startup investments, including some milestone "exits," which
Kristina will reveal in the chapters ahead. I've been hon-
ored to collaborate with JumpFund on events, including
returning to Tennessee to speak at a reception for local en-
trepreneurs and investors at the 36|86 startup conference
in 2017 and sharing the story of Kristina and her intrepid
partners when I have presented to crowds across the U.S.
from SXSW to Google to UBS to BNY Mellon.

When JumpFund first started a decade ago, Kristina
and her cohort faced pushback and the questions: "Why
women? Why now?" As you'll read in the chapters ahead,

the sisterhood shaking up tech in Chattanooga ultimately answered these queries with results. Their resounding success demonstrates how investing in women drives both innovation and the bottom line. And perhaps it will inspire you, dear reader, to jump in, too!

—Heather Cabot, January 2024
Author, *Geek Girl Rising* (2017), *The New Chardonnay* (2020), and *Level Up* (2022), with Stacey Abrams and Laura Hodgson

Prologue

On a June day in 2019, I stood on the edge of an inflatable dinghy in the middle of the Arctic Ocean in a bathing suit, teeth chattering and heart racing. A crowd stood above me on the ship, cheering me on. My head screamed, *This is crazy!* My heart, however, said, *Let's do this!*

Against all rational thought, I took the leap into the 28-degree waters, surrounded by Arctic polar ice caps. Stung and briefly immobilized by the intensity of the cold, I felt motionless for a few seconds under the water, watching the bubbles rise around me surrounded by a deep, cold silence. Shocked back into consciousness, I quickly resurfaced and strong arms pulled me up and out, wrapping me in warm towels. Back inside the ship, I cheered and celebrated with other brave souls, revitalized with shots of vodka and chasers of warm blueberry soup.

Just an hour before my polar plunge, I had decided to join a stalwart group of passengers on the National Geographic Explorer for this Arctic rite of passage. Global warming has not yet changed the fact that the Arctic Ocean is still below-freezing. For this act of thrilling insanity, I proudly earned a badge with an image of a woman jumping into a similar frozen sea. In front of me, two visiting teachers had jumped in with festive Narwhal hats, full of smiles one minute and shaking to their core the next. My mother, who was celebrating her 75th birthday and had always wanted to see the beauty and fragility of the Arctic, cheered me on with the rest of the passengers above deck.

The knowledge that others were there to support me and we were all doing this personal challenge together made it feel less risky.

This story of jumping into something daunting is at the heart of why we started our first angel investment fund composed of women investing in women ten years ago. We wanted a title that addressed the confidence necessary to launch into something unknown and risky, yet potentially rewarding. "Just jump in" became our group's rallying cry and motivation to other women, be they investors or entrepreneurs. We wanted to encourage more women to lean into the unknown, move beyond the safety and comfort of their current realities, and cannonball into something new and exciting, and potentially lucrative and transformative.

This is a story about standing on the edge of that precipice, facing a great unknown, a scary, risky endeavor, but ready to take the leap because you know deep in your heart it's right and will make you feel proud you made a difference. Women face layered challenges in work and life—bias, sexism, childcare, financial constraints—which makes starting a company a more complicated, scary business. Investing in startup ventures is also risky and many women have not leveraged their assets in this way so it is wholly unknown territory. The founders of JumpFund wanted to show that we understood the tug between heart and mind. We wanted to challenge the limiting beliefs many women, including ourselves, may have about money and success and just do it. Launch it. Start it. Invest in it.

This is the story of leaving a top job at the pinnacle of your original career, to leap with utter faith and conviction into a completely unknown field. A story of seven badass women who leveraged all of their resources—time, talent, and treasure—to impact a small corner of an industry historically dominated by men. A story of mission-driven work to fundamentally change the status quo. A story of creating safe spaces, the opportunity to learn and grow, and lean into a support network of like-minded women (and a few good men) well beyond our own backyard. This is the story of "jumping in," with head and heart, and making a real difference for other women.

This is a story for anyone looking to invest in a company with the values and leadership that you want to see perpetuated in the world. For those who believe that:

→ Your investments can make an impact AND a return.
→ The collective power of women can move mountains.
→ We must work to level the vastly unfair playing field women still face.
→ Together we can make a difference and change the game for women entrepreneurs.
→ Paying it forward is not only important, but the right thing to do and will reap manifold rewards.
→ And by doing so, you can feel good about the time, money, and talent you spent.

I invite everyone to jump in—the water is invigorating, and rejuvenating, and the ripple effects are manifold.

Introduction

She believed she could, so she did. —R.S. Grey

My intention with this book is twofold. The first is to share our story about jumping into this whole new world of angel investing with a passion to correct the significant imbalance in access to capital for female entrepreneurs. The second is to serve as a guide for other women curious to learn about this asset class and possibly be ready to take the plunge themselves to run their own angel investing network or fund. From the beginning, JumpFund has been honest and transparent about our own journeys and has tried to share our new knowledge about the world of venture capital, its language, methods, process, approach, and pitfalls. We embraced a collective "learning by doing" model and included both our investors and entrepreneurs in this process.

As I often like to say, angel investing is not "rocket science." But its complexity lies in the nuance of relationships, the building of trust, and working together to support successful companies that will make a return and an impact. By creating your own tribe and surrounding yourself with strong partners who all bring their own areas of expertise to the table, the work is lighter and not so daunting. We have much more work to do and need many more women (and good men) engaged in supporting the success of female founders and impact-driven companies.

Our ultimate vision in launching JumpFund was "to make the Southeast the BEST place for a woman to invest in or build a business." We have since proven this thesis by recruiting more than one hundred women, the majority of whom had not previously been angel investors, to invest in women-led startups in our region. And our portfolio of investments in over thirty women-led companies clearly indicates that the deal flow of strong, investable, female founders exists in the Southeast.

In this book, you will learn how and why we built our own startup angel fund and how you might do the same, or at least join the growing ranks of women investing in women. This book is intended to serve as an encouragement to other women curious about investing in early stage companies and how the power of our purse can radically shift how capital flows to woefully underrepresented founders. Reading our story and examples of other women engaged in this field, you will learn:

→ How seven women in a mid-sized Southern city started their own angel fund.
→ What is angel investing and why we need more women angels.
→ The importance of investing with a gender lens.
→ The basics of finding and investing in early stage, women-led startups.
→ How other women are growing the number and impact of women angel investors.

Why Women?

Frankly, I get weary of answering this question in every interview, panel, or discussion with other early stage investors. Why *not* women? Women make up over half the global population and start more than 40% of new businesses in the U.S. every year. Women like Sarah Blakely, who bootstrapped her own body shapewear company SPANX into a billion-dollar venture. Women like Whitney Wolfe, who raised over $2.2B and launched the initial public offering (IPO) of the dating app Bumble. Women like Carol Tomé, who jump started UPS's flatlined stock after taking over during a global pandemic. These are just three badass women who have started or successfully led, high growth companies. These stories of successful women-led ventures are becoming more common. And they are just the tip of the iceberg.

In her book *Financial Feminism*, Jessica Robinson highlights evidence-based research on the economic benefits of women as business leaders. Companies in the top quartile for gender diversity on their executive teams were 21% more likely to experience above average profitability than companies in the fourth quartile, according to a McKinsey study on diversity and corporate performance. An S&P study found that firms with female CEOs and CFOs produced superior stock price performance, compared with the market average, and in 24 months post-appointment, female CEOs saw a 20% stock price increase and female CFOs a 6% increase in profitability and 8% greater stock returns. MSCI found that U.S. companies with at least three women on their boards had a median increase of 37% per share and 10% ROE (return on equity) over a 5-year period.[1]

The JumpFund saw these economic markers as yet more evidence for why we needed to start our own fund to invest in women. By planting a flag firmly in our Southeast U.S. soil and sending out a beacon to all female entrepreneurs in an eight-state radius, JumpFund opened a floodgate of eager founders seeking capital where none had been readily accessible before. We were out to prove that we could produce strong "deal flow" (the number of quality deals an investor reviews) and thus find high quality, overlooked companies in which to invest.

In other words, we saw a HUGE opportunity, even if we were narrowing our scope to only women in a particular region of the U.S. Since this particular group of entrepreneurs had traditionally bootstrapped their way to success we actually saw this as arbitrage, where we had access to deals other investors were blithely passing by even though they were right under their noses. We were also encouraged that our gendered approach attracted more diversity across the board, with companies led by people of color, LGBTQ+ founders as well as mixed gender teams. There was truly a wealth of opportunity out there, not a deficit, and we continue to see this strong deal flow replicated with other funds and angel networks investing with a gender lens or seeking more diversity on founding teams.

Our startup story and the stories of other women like us inspired me to write this book. Those who have seen the huge disparities in access to capital for female founders and launched their own groups of women to invest in other women. Our story is hopefully just the beginning of a chapter in which gender lens investing becomes mainstream and capital is more equitably accessible for all entrepreneurs. Entrepreneurism is a key driver of our economy and until women have the same opportunities to pursue their startup dreams we will never reach economic parity. So, read on and consider how you too might jump in.

Stage Fright

There have been many studies on why women resist the pull of entrepreneurship as well as early stage investing. To me, the "fear factor" inherent in both of these risky endeavors seems to be a major reason. And it is not that women cannot overcome their fears and take the risk necessary to jump in, it is that many of us are much more methodical and deliberate in our approach to new and scary things. We have more confidence in taking risks if we feel we are prepared and grounded in the material and can step into the ring with at least a basic knowledge of what we are getting into.

This may seem antithetical to risk taking, as risk is often thought of as stepping into the unknown, diving headfirst into those cold, icy Arctic waters with blind faith. Yet for me, I have always balanced my fear with ample preparation and as many tools in my toolbox as possible before I do something that scares or intimidates me. For most of my early life, I wanted to be an actress when I grew up. I started acting when I was in elementary school at a local children's theater and caught the bug. In high school and college, I continued to pursue my thespian passion but put it on hold when I stepped into my first career in education.

When my first child was a toddler, I decided to step back onto the stage through the portal of community theater. It was much more terrifying as an adult, putting oneself out there, fears, anxiety, and all, in full view of your peers. But there is something inside me that innately loves the risk, the rush I get from stepping into a completely other character than myself and entertaining people.

I also know though that I cannot step onstage unprepared. I spend countless hours learning lines, considering how this character would deliver them, and how to be this person onstage. The first thing people who have not acted before ask when they have seen you onstage in a big role is, "How did you learn all those lines?" And yes, that is certainly part of it. But it's not about rote delivery in acting, churning out words from a page, it's about how you deliver those lines and become the character that speaks them. That is the larger fear for the actor, how we will be portrayed by the audience. Are we any good, or just a terrible hack?

Being onstage will always be one of the most fear invoking yet joyful things I have done. The feeling of standing on that precipice, behind a stage door, ready to take a huge leap of faith with an audience. Deep breathing and infinite preparation have helped me through these moments, as well as an underlying confidence in myself that at that very moment, even though I seem to have forgotten ALL my lines just before I step out, they will come rushing back to me as I inhabit the character onstage, whoever she may be.

As an actor, there is also a large amount of trust placed in your fellow cast members. Although they are all facing their own fears as they step onstage, you need to know they will be able to shepherd you if you stumble. The knowledge and comfort that they have done their own homework, as evidenced in long hours of rehearsals and run-throughs, is what often carries you forward in a show –the back and forth of dialogue, action, and reaction to others in this intimate world you have created.

What does this all have to do with angel investing and supporting entrepreneurs? As women, we need to learn a new script to be able to walk onto the stage as an investor. There is a whole other language and posture required for this work that may be foreign to some of us, it certainly was to me. For many of us, it is strange to be on the side of the table that holds the purse strings as we have spent many years as volunteers or leaders in organizations asking for money to support our causes. And as with most industries, there is lingo and a basic playbook that is all part of the drama. In the first year or two as active angel investors, our general partners and I embraced an attitude of "fake it til you make it" as we felt we were drinking from a firehose of knowledge and best practices. Yet, as with anything you rehearse over time and build your confidence in, it becomes easier to play the role.

The term "angel investor" actually stems from the early days of Broadway. Investors, also known as producers, of Broadway shows were considered to be the "angels" whose investment helped undergird their potential success. As we know, a Broadway caliber production can be a hit or a big flop, which meant investing in this "asset" was extremely risky and required a deep love of theater and its potential for strong returns if a show returned great reviews. Broadway angel investors also often paid forward any positive returns on their investments into future shows, becoming serial producers.

I have never been wholly averse to risk, just cautious in my approach, and a perfectionist by nature. I find this is also true with other women. Men in this industry are seen as big, bold risk takers, both as investors and entrepreneurs. For some, angel investing is akin to gambling and playing a high stakes game. For others, it's a show of bravado and ego, backing those in which they see their younger selves. Women tend to be more deliberate, gathering all the information, studying their lines, and polishing their practice until they feel confident to venture forth and commit their capital. We certainly did this as JumpFund founding partners, spending time with Golden Seeds and other advisors in the space, watching and learning from them before placing our first bets. Education and mentorship are key, as it's best to rehearse alongside others until you are comfortable taking the stage on your own.

Given my lifelong love of the stage and the appetite for risk that is inherent in acting, this book is divided into "Acts" each with its own theme and focus. They are not progressive as in a play but do build on each other. Take them on their own or find the Acts that resonate with you. From the inspiration of our JumpFund story, to how to get started in angel investing or launching your own fund, to finding yourself in other women who are actively investing in other women and "growing our own," I hope you find motivation to join us in this important work.

ACT I

Jumping In

1

Jumping In

At the end of the day, money is the real key to gender equality.

—Sally Krawcheck, Founder, Ellevest

Wakeup Call

In the spring of 2013, I sat in my University office with a young woman, full of hope and ambition about her idea for her own startup venture. Yet, I also remember the frustration and anger this young business student shared with me about the reception she was receiving in our local entrepreneurial ecosystem for her nascent business idea, a new concept for reducing excessive plastic packaging of organic cleaning products (think bulk foods with reusable containers). When she asked about resources in our community to help get her off the starting block, I suggested she explore a new company incubator program that hosted a "48 hour launch" each year. This program was designed to spend two full days (day and night) "hacking" your business idea surrounded by mentors with legal, marketing, finance, business strategy, and pitch experience. At the end of the process, each entrepreneur in the program pitches their business idea to compete for prize money to help launch their venture.

When I mentioned the incubator program she surprisingly told me she had already had conversations with the group hosting the event and that she didn't feel it was a right fit. The incubator space was ripe with 20-something, tech savvy young (mostly white) men, hacking away in a tight, shared office space with their headphones on, hammering out their own genius business concepts. She had met with several well-meaning coaches there but she did not feel comfortable or supported in the incubator's predominantly male environment. She had been told her idea did not really have legs. I was shocked to hear this as I knew those who ran the program and felt they all had the best intentions and would provide an open door to any entrepreneur. But, perception is often reality and this confident young woman was clearly feeling that this was not the right place for her to further explore her business idea.

During my tenure as an Assistant Dean at the University of Tennessee at Chattanooga's Rollins College of Business, I often met with individual students as they forged their career paths or looked for mentors and advisors in their area of business. One of the aspects of my job I enjoyed the most was teaching the capstone Senior Seminar on career success and coaching students as they explored their career options. Many students were interested in entrepreneurship or had dreams of one day launching their own ventures, even if they were starting out in corporate environments.

Our entrepreneurial program had only recently added "pitch competitions" and courses focused on business idea pitch preparation. This young woman in my office was looking to take the next step toward launching her business by extending her network, as I fervently encouraged students to do in my Senior Seminar course. She had gingerly dipped her toe in the burgeoning ecosystem Chattanooga was just beginning to launch to support high growth startups, and found the waters foreboding and icy cold.

This meeting was a wakeup call for me. I had been coaching all students to build their social and professional networks, reach beyond the University's doors to connect with Chattanooga's business community and position themselves well to launch their business careers in our mid-sized city. I was appalled and frustrated that female students in particular might be experiencing bias and feel unwelcome when we had forged so many strong relationships and the business community was actively recruiting our students for top jobs. What was I to tell this eager, smart young woman ready to pursue her startup venture? With no startup space that felt welcoming and no role models in our ecosystem, the prospects seemed bleak. Our burgeoning startup community seemed to be built by men for men. What was going on in our city that we were still perpetuating age-old bias and a good ol' boy mentality while promoting an innovative, entrepreneurial business environment?

Gig City

By 2013, Chattanooga was fast becoming a mecca for young creatives and the entrepreneurial minded. We were the first city in the U.S. to build a high-speed, gigabit fiber optic network hosted by our Electric Power Board (EPB) and thus rebranded as the Gig City. Well before Google Fiber or big cities attempting to address an overloaded internet, Chattanooga was streaming a gig to local homes and up to ten times that to local businesses. EPB quickly realized the asset they had created, spurred by a desire to create a more sustainable electric infrastructure that was not as susceptible to power outages caused by intense, seasonal storms. And, along with the Chattanooga Chamber and others, began to promote this new high-speed access widely.

It was a heady time for Chattanooga. Volkswagen recently built its first North American plant in our backyard, tapping into state and local government tax incentives. Our downtown was in the midst of a major revitalization, with public/private partnerships rethinking our Main Street all the way to the Tennessee River. An influx of new housing, schools, and urban infill of shops, restaurants, and green spaces began to reshape our city's landscape.

Our local economic development think tank, the Enterprise Center, along with foundations and city government, began to focus efforts on how our city attracts and retains talent as well as new business. Chattanooga was known predominantly as a manufacturing town and our city's leadership was looking for ways we could rebrand as a regional innovation hub. A recently created startup incubator, the Company Lab (Co.Lab), had been spawned a few years prior by an effort called Create Here, to envision a future Chattanooga which might be a beacon for young entrepreneurs and creatives. The siren song of the startup economy powered by high speed internet was beginning to make Chattanooga a hotspot in the Southeast for those who were interested in starting or growing a tech-based venture.

Yet, in the first few years of its development, our startup economy was predominantly white and very much all-male. This included the leadership of our accelerators, the startup companies recruited to Chattanooga through a "GigTank" pitch competition, and even the activity going on at the state level with Launch Tennessee, a statewide initiative to support entrepreneurship and drive more localized investment. Every demo stage, the pitch judges, and audiences of potential investors were filled with men. New startups popping up around Chattanooga were all led by young, ambitious men, with offices that sported beer bars, foosball tables, gaming rooms, and a definitively "bro" culture.

To discuss the clear diversity deficit in our entrepreneurial ecosystem a group of women gathered in a conference room at the LampPost Group, a new venture incubator. Called together by LampPost's only female partner,

Shelley Prevost, and serial entrepreneur Tiffanie Robinson, we met to discuss the lack of women we were seeing both as early stage investors as well as pitching startups on our local demo stages. Even at LampPost, where up to ten companies shared workspace to further develop their ventures while receiving coaching and capital, the teams were 99% male.

The women attending those first meetings included leaders in banking and finance, marketing, media, small business development, and nonprofits as well as accountants, lawyers, entrepreneurs, and philanthropists. The conversation at these gatherings focused on the concerns and issues we were witnessing and in some cases living, but solutions were not readily forthcoming. We had a robust women's leadership network in our community, the Chattanooga Women's Leadership Institute, with a focus on supporting women at all stages of their careers, including women launching new businesses. A philanthropic Women's Fund had recently formed to address socio-economic policy issues at the state and local level impacting women. Mentors and support groups for women in business, from accounting to tech, were plenty in our community but why were women entrepreneurs still not being seen or heard from?

In our shiny, new Gig City, business incubators and accelerators were dominated by male founders, mentors, and investors. Much like my business school student, young women often did not feel comfortable discussing their nascent business ideas in this environment feeling that they might be belittled or told they did not have what it takes to be a successful entrepreneur. At UT Chattanooga, the female entrepreneurship or finance majors were outnumbered by their male peers. For many of them, this was seen as a challenge, a glass ceiling to break. "Lean in," they were told, don't take no for an answer. Live your full potential and "give it all you've got." But that is a difficult prospect when you constantly feel there are no safe spaces or support systems to help you realize your dreams.

Was this a problem unique to our southern, "good old boy" city or something bigger? Who else was seeing this problem and what were others doing about it? Much like good entrepreneurs, hungry for a solution, we set about trying to find out.

Where are the Women?

A few months after my wake-up call to the gender silos in our Gig City, and the series of meetings Shelley and Tiffanie had hosted with local women on how to address the gap in our entrepreneurial ecosystem for female founders, another gathering took place. Company pitches had been going on throughout the day for a culmination of "Gig-Tank," our city's version of Y Combinator, where young, entrepreneurial gladiators pitch their companies to a group of judges and throngs of local ecosystem supporters. In a side room off the main stage at GigTank a small group was gathered in response to a call for a discussion about the lack of diversity we had just witnessed on stage.

This lively "sidebar" discussion was attended by several women leaders from Shelley and Tiffanie's roundtables, including myself, as well as two women from the West Coast who were visiting as pitch competition judges and two men (brave souls). We were seeking solutions to what evidently was an issue not just in the Southeast, but a phenomenon these west coasters were seeing in similar entrepreneurial support programs across the country. Where were the women?

We were told by these visiting female pitch judges that to challenge this male-dominated landscape, CAPITAL was the key. They were beginning to see efforts in Silicon Valley to address the issue of gender parity in startup ecosystems and increasing access to capital was paramount. They told us that research had shown that less than 3% of venture capital (early stage funding for startup ventures) was going to women-led companies in the U.S. This was a startling figure. If we could activate a pool of venture capital that invested specifically in female-led ventures, that would be a game changer.

At GigTank, we had watched a stage full of men pitch their nascent ventures, who would likely all go on to secure funding. There were even local funders teed up to provide seed capital to promising companies, especially if they chose to stay and build their businesses in Chattanooga. If we could harness capital solely directed to female founders, we might be able to put more women on those stages and help them secure additional investment. Capital is critical for an early stage venture, giving it the wings to take off and grow. If the ecosystem we currently had was not attracting or funding women-led ventures, maybe we needed to grow and fund our own portfolio of companies.

It was also becoming clear to us that the lack of women in our entrepreneurial ecosystem was not just a problem in our backyard, but much more widespread. Several of us who were thinking deeply about this issue began to attend other regional "demo days" to see if the landscape looked different beyond our city. One of the first we attended was hosted by Launch Tennessee, a newly formed statewide economic development organization dedicated to advancing entrepreneurship and early stage investment in Tennessee. At their inaugural demo day in Nashville, we counted a total of five women in the audience of over 400 attendees, which included me and Shelley. The other women included Lisa Calhoun, who later went on to launch Valor Ventures in Atlanta, and Fran Marcum of Marcum Capital as well as one of Shelley's female summer interns from LampPost. That was it. Not a single woman pitched on stage that day, and in fact all of the presenters were white men save for one Asian-American man. All of the judges were also men, along with the other investors and network supporters in the audience.

We were both shocked and emboldened. How could a *statewide* pitch competition not showcase more diversity? Why was this an almost 99% male audience? Again, where were the women? Armed with the knowledge that capital could be a critical component in answering this question and altering the landscape for female entrepreneurs, we decided to jump in.

Taking the Leap

At this point, our small but mighty band of women knew two things. First, we were not seeing women on these demo stages, in our local entrepreneurial ecosystem, or even regionally in accelerators and incubator programs. Second, we were also not seeing any women engaged as early stage investors.

But it was conversations with our male counterparts in local angel funds and capital networks that really put a chip on our shoulders and made us lean in to start our own fund created by women for women. Early on in our exploration phase of how to start a fund to invest in women-led ventures, we looked to others in our ecosystem for guidance and best practices. We had been learning the lingo of early stage investing and understood that those who are often the first to invest in a company, after friends and family, are referred to as angel investors. Some of these angels invest directly into companies on their own, while others choose to invest alongside a group of like-minded individuals either in a member network or through a dedicated fund.

Doing our homework, we began to meet with leaders

(always all-male) of local angel groups investing in early stage startups in our region. In one particular meeting, it was suggested that a solely female-focused fund would likely not be successful since these investors had little if any female founders in their pipeline of potential companies. From their experience, investable women-led companies just did not exist or "they would have seen them." They considered themselves gender agnostic with an "open door" to any entrepreneur. They even went so far as to relate that they had been pitched, by a man, for a feminine hygiene product which they had to ask one of their sisters to evaluate as they didn't have the "expertise."

These comments of course made us even more determined to start an angel fund of our own. Even without fully testing the waters, we knew there were female founders out there starting growth ventures in the Southeast. A new accelerator program focused on female founders was starting up in Memphis and we had witnessed significant activity in Atlanta, including entrepreneurial pitch events hosted by Sarah Blakely, founder of SPANX. Deal flow did exist that was ripe for investment even if these female founders were not on the radar of most traditional investors.

This group of men also told us that it would be difficult for us to source other women to invest in a fund dedicated to women. In their opinion, there were no other "women like us" who would want to invest in this often risky and generally unknown asset class of angel investing. Their experience was that most women followed their husband's advice on investing and they had only been able to ever recruit one woman to invest in their fund, a local doctor with her own practice. For some reason they did not know any women who had control of their own assets or would be interested in the high risk, high reward world of early stage company investing.

To some extent they were right. Although we did not yet know it, at the time we started our first fund in 2013, less than 5% of women were angel investors. Still less were partners in venture capital firms. But even back then, the number was growing. Golden Seeds, the largest and earliest network of women angel investors in the country, have been at the forefront of recruiting women to invest in other women since 2005. They had witnessed a significant rise in women engaged in angel investing and consequently women entrepreneurs receiving funding for their early stage ventures. According to Golden Seeds founding partner, Loretta McCarthy, "the growth in the number of women investors since 2004 coincides with a period of time in which women—in large numbers—have recognized they have the skills, interests, networks and capital to invest in ways that did not previously exist."

From those first meetings at GigTank and with other local funds, we clearly understood that we were the women who had the skills, interests, networks and capital to invest. And that we all knew other "women like us" we felt would also be interested in this value proposition. So, with no experience as early stage investors, we set out to explore what starting an angel fund and raising capital was all about.

Fund Modeling

As we sought mentors for creating an angel fund, the Chattanooga Renaissance Fund (CRF) was our nearest role model as JumpFund began to take shape. The founders of CRF had started their locally focused fund only a few years earlier on the premise that new technology companies were being drawn to Chattanooga with our gigabit infrastructure and high potential, early stage investments were surfacing from local incubator programs such as LampPost Group and our Company Lab. Their fund's mission was to invest primarily in Chattanooga-based companies at a "seed" capital level to help them launch and grow to garner next stage growth capital. CRF truly saw a renaissance taking place in Chattanooga and a clear investment opportunity alongside.

Following CRF's lead, we saw how a mission-oriented angel investment fund worked and liked the model. Their first fund was approximately $3mm and we were considering $2.5mm which seemed like an appropriate first marker to test the local pulse of female investors We had also begun talking with other early stage investment groups which had more of a "network" model, where investors pay a membership fee to gain access to interesting investment opportunities and then pool their capital to invest in a potential business venture. We did not relish the idea of "herding the cats" each time we found a company worthy of investment nor keeping momentum going among investors who may or may not be fully engaged or interested in the deep diligence needed to vet each opportunity as often happens with angel networks.

Since we had yet to prove out the deal flow of women-led companies in the Southeast and the influx of capital we might be able to initially capture, we decided that a fund model was more suited to our interests and abilities. Angel funds pool investors' capital to invest in a portfolio of companies instead of writing individual checks and are often managed by a general partner. Our vision was simple yet revolutionary at the time – harness women's capital to invest in women-led businesses in the Southeast.

48 Hour Launch: Female Founders Edition

First, we had to see if there really were women-led ventures that were hungry to pitch their businesses. Our local Company Lab (Co.Lab), an accelerator for high growth startups, had hosted a 48 Hour Launch program for several years. We had noticed they had very women participants, with the exception of Tiffanie Robinson, one of our future JumpFund partners, who was young and hungry and not intimidated by the "Cheeto-eating boys" with whom she found herself surrounded.[2] Co.Lab was also the startup support organization which had turned off the young female entrepreneur I had counseled at UTC. So, we approached Co.Lab with the idea of running an all-female 48 Hour Launch, complete with childcare, which we knew would be a gamechanger for women who had a business idea but maybe not the time dedicated to exploring it.

Initially, we were met with a lukewarm response from Co.Lab and an "if you build it let's see if they come" attitude. They did not believe there were truly that many women in our community who would want to participate, as they had previously had very few female applicants. But the nonprofit organization and its leadership were definitely interested in diversifying their pool of startup founders so let us give it a go.

Well, we built it and they did come. We had 24 applicants for the first Female Founder 48 Hour Launch, on par with other Co.Lab programs, of which we chose ten for the cohort. One woman, a mom of four (going on five), was thrilled to have childcare as she told us she had wanted to participate in the past but had never been able to since her husband also worked full time. She had also never had a babysitter! Other women thanked us for the opportunity to explore their business ideas in a safe environment where they felt more comfortable sharing their ideas and working with other women.

The companies ranged from a monthly subscription box for moms (run by the mother of four who was also a behavioral psychologist) to a beauty company geared to helping women "rock their red" by finding the best shade of lipstick to boost their self-esteem. Though no revolutionary technology companies were in the first cohort, the women who participated were serious about creating ventures that could grow and succeed. Like any entrepreneur in a good business incubator, they benefited greatly from the headspace to create and collaborate with designers, marketers, legal, business strategists, and potential investors to help them build their company's pitch. After 48 hours, the women rocked that demo stage and set a new precedent for how Co.Lab recruited and ran its programs to be more inclusive and supportive of women.

At the Female Founder 48 hour launch we unveiled our own concept and new name, The JumpFund—an investment fund built by women for women. Behind the scenes, we had been working on our branding and pitch. Tiffanie had the brilliant idea to name this new venture Jump-Fund, challenging the notion that women are risk-averse and sending a message that we support female founders "taking the plunge" and starting their own businesses. She thought of all the times she had stood at the edge, daring herself to take the leap into the unknown. The name and image resonated with all of us and we jumped in with our first investments of cash prizes to the winners of the Female Founder 48 Hour Launch. The newly formed Jump-Fund had its first win and we were off to the races.

Since then, JumpFund has invested in over thirty women-led ventures from a pool of hundreds of applications and referrals from across the Southeast. We had not only found "women like us" to invest, but we had opened the floodgates to a robust flow of women-led companies in our region who had finally found "friendly" investors to consider their ventures. We likened ourselves to a Dolphin Tank vs. Shark Tank, where we prodded and nudged companies during pitches and beyond, wanting to be an open door for women-led ventures who had only had doors closed on them in the past. We hosted educational sessions on angel investing for our limited partners, women who were new to this asset class. We brought in other women who were investing in early stage, women-led companies and discussed how they conducted due diligence, fund management, and built supportive relationships with their portfolio companies. And we launched an annual Southeast Women's Venture Summit to gather our founders and investors for rich conversations and potential further investment in these growing ventures. We took the plunge and have been surprised and encouraged by the ripple effect we created throughout the Southeast and beyond.

ACT II

Making the Dream Work

2

Making the Dream Work

Who you are surrounded by often determines who you become.

—Vicky Saunders, Founder, SheEO

Building Our Badass Tribe

Like any successful startup, building the right founding team is key to your success. Solo founders often hit a wall when they don't have others to help carry the load and add alternative viewpoints, sharing their expertise and strategic direction. It was clear that those of us who had been leading the charge on community conversations about access to capital for women would all be part of our core team. Shelley Prevost, Tiffanie Robinson, Stefanie Crowe and I were the initial co-founders and hosted the first conversations about developing our own investment vehicle for women-led ventures.

As a twenty-year career educator, I knew we needed to build a strong leadership bench with deep business experience to launch our own angel investment fund. I am the first to admit that I do not have the traditional finance or business background of most angel fund leaders and I knew these skills would be important on our team. We needed both the expertise and credibility to indicate to investors that although we were first-time fund managers, we had the skills to vet successful investments and manage a portfolio of companies to bring strong returns. I also knew that women angel investors were few and far between in those early days of 2013, especially in our region, so we needed to find other women who "got it" and were willing to learn what was needed to build a fund.

Working with a friendly and supportive legal team we formed our first Limited Liability Company or LLC (the management group) and Limited Partnership (the investment partnership) entities. Shelley, Tiffanie and I knew we wanted to expand our initial General Partner group that would manage the fund, so we invited Betsy Brown, manager of a local trust company and Cory Allison, a serial entrepreneur and eager investor wanting to "pay it forward" for other women entrepreneurs. And, as we launched Fund II, Kim Seals, a former HR executive turned avid angel investor whom we had met through our early days at Golden Seeds, joined our managing team and became our anchor in the hot Atlanta market. Leonora Williamson, a Harvard Business School educated consultant was also with us the first few years and added great value, but later exited the fund and now serves as a business consultant and coach in Nashville. This core group is what truly gave JumpFund its backbone and heft to leverage our first $2.5mm fund, raised solely from women in Chattanooga. Our investors were betting on us as community leaders they trusted and felt had the expertise to pull off this new venture.

The original founders of JumpFund spanned the gamut of experience and achievement. All were badass women, as we coined ourselves and our future investors. Shelley had a front row seat to the gender bias present in venture capital. As she coached young startup teams through the early growing pains of building their companies at Lamp-Post, she was conscious that she was often the only woman in the room. In fact, she often felt like her role was that of a mother to these young male founders. As a psychologist she could help entrepreneurs navigate the often turbulent, emotional roller coaster of launching a startup venture. But it became clear that these teams might be stronger and understand their broader market opportunity if they were more diverse.

Tiffanie was a serial entrepreneur turned commercial real estate maven with a passion for revitalizing Chattanooga's downtown core. At the time of JumpFund's launch, she was working with RiverCity Company, a woman-led public-private organization dedicated to bringing back Chattanooga's downtown and filling empty buildings in our downtown core. Chattanooga's renaissance over the past thirty years was in part due to environmental clean up and as well as a concerted effort by local leaders to reinvest in their city and make it an exciting place to live and work. Through her work with RiverCity, Tiffanie helped attract new businesses to our downtown and reanimated underutilized real estate. She and her husband even launched one of their own businesses, a savory and sweet pie shop, in the heart of the city.

Through her work with local businesses, Tiffanie also was seeing a lack of support for female leaders and business owners. As an entrepreneur herself, she was one of the only women who had participated in the Company Lab's original 48 hour launch. Yet she was frustrated that more women were not involved and the program certainly had no support systems such as childcare to help make it easier for women to participate. Working with an all female group at the RiverCity Company, she was emboldened to find a better, more supportive path for women entrepreneurs in Chattanooga.

Stefanie Crowe was another key JumpFund founder. With Shelley and Tiffanie, our founding team had strong experience working with and understanding entrepreneurs. Stefanie, with a twenty year career in banking, brought an important financial perspective and experience to our nascent fund. Stefanie's leadership role at a de novo bank (which later went on to be acquired by

Pinnacle Financial) clearly understood the investor side of the table, having worked for years as a wealth advisor with many high net worth women. She not only brought interested potential investors to the fund, but helped us craft our messaging on the value proposition of women investing in women. She understood that this was not just about a philanthropic "pay it forward" proposition, but a market opportunity of which few other investors were taking advantage. She also had personally experienced significant gender bias in the banking and financial field, fighting her way to positions of leadership and constantly reminding even her newly formed bank, which purported to be "different" and more progressive, that women's voices and presence were needed at all levels if they were to be successful.

Once this core team was formed, we discussed who else might be a right fit to round out our General Partner team. We knew we needed to bring additional key financial and business knowledge to the table to further legitimize our effort. I had met Betsy Brown through our local downtown Rotary, one of the largest and oldest in the Southeast, though a decidedly "good old boy" network that had only allowed women to join in 1991 and did not have a woman president until 2009. While I did not know Betsy well, I did know she was well respected in the local business community as a trust officer and former banker, having built deep relationships as a wealth advisor to many prominent families and business leaders. We were thrilled that Betsy's interest peaked when we discussed the prospect of building an all women-led, women focused fund. Her perspective on our pitch to investors, from her background working with high net worth families and particularly women and their estates, was invaluable. Betsy's extensive network beyond Chattanooga also helped us eventually expand our fundraising with a wider regional and national network.

To round out the group, we added the help of Leonora Williamson, a transplant to Chattanooga from the Northeast, and Harvard Business School alum. Leonora had been a business strategist for several local companies and she helped us again hone our pitch and lean into the value proposition of investing in diverse teams. And finally, Cory Allison, another serial entrepreneur and fellow Washington and Lee alumni of Betsy's, came knocking on my door one day. I had known Cory from her local baby and children's store, Wiggle Worm, which she had successfully grown and recently sold. She had heard through the grapevine that we were launching a fund and she wanted in. I was thrilled to have another investor materialize out of the blue and was excited to have Cory engaged in our fund. But after she walked out the door of our office, she literally walked right back in and said that beyond investing, what she really wanted was to be part of our leadership team! Since then, Cory has been one of our staunchest supporters and cheerleaders and an important member of our general partner team.

In the book *Geek Girl Rising* (2017) by Heather Cabot, profiling women in tech and the rise of women angels funding them, JumpFund is featured in a section titled "Badass Investors Beyond Silicon Valley." In her research on a visit to Chattanooga, Heather found that our investors were predominantly banking on the founding partner team leading JumpFund. As Cathy Boettner, one of our early investors states in the book, "there are badass women in Chattanooga and they own it. They don't apologize for it, they don't hide from it … and it's not in an arrogant or snotty way, it's just they are who they are, and I love that."[3] Akin to how we judge the background of founding startup teams, our investors weighed our collective expertise and proven leadership abilities as markers of future success.

Our badassery became our moniker. We wanted to disrupt and challenge the status quo and do something bold and new, at least for the Southeast. We were certainly the vanguards in our region, as no other women-led, female founder focused, early stage investment group existed and we were forging a path all on our own. Our investors knew this and were excited to join our effort to change the landscape and start something that could have real impact for women economically and socially.

United in our mission to prove that the Southeast had women-led ventures in which to invest as well as women's capital eager to deploy, we moved forward building our first fund. We quickly realized though that with all of us in full time leadership positions we did not have anyone to steer the ship. I had been in my position as Assistant Dean at UT Chattanooga's business school for three years at that point, which I like to say afforded me a business degree by osmosis. At UTC, I led our PR and marketing, fundraised, and worked closely with a new Dean on vision and strategy. I also helped launch several successful auxiliary programs during my tenure, including a Veterans Entrepreneurship Program and Finance for the Future, a program focused on identifying and recruiting more women in finance. My role also included mentoring business students both in our undergraduate and graduate programs, particularly around career pathways and helping them connect with internships and jobs in our community.

I was excited and passionate about my work at the business school, but the nascent idea of harnessing capital to support more women in business was a magnetic call to action. I have always been a passionate advocate for women and an avowed feminist. I do not shy away from that moniker, and rather have always embraced it even as I've spent over half of my life in the South (emigrating from Seattle by way of New York) where feminism is sometimes a dirty word or a leftist, liberal label. I believe in women's equality in all things and feel any woman should have the opportunity to fulfill her dreams on equal par with men. I have a daughter and a son who I raised to be staunch allies for women's rights and a husband who supports everything I do and is a champion for equity on many fronts. I also understand my deep privilege as a white woman who has always had the resources and opportunity to pursue her passions. I want to use these tools and resources to help other women have the same confidence and access I have been afforded and someday be able to "pay it forward" themselves.

With this deep-seated calling, I knew I was the one who could both afford to and wanted to take the leap and jump headlong into launching an angel fund. While it was bittersweet parting from a job that I loved, the idea of starting something completely new and challenging norms and existing structures was exhilarating. I was also offered a space to headquarter our fund as well as back office support from our family office. I truly do not know if Jump-Fund would have ever taken off were it not for their support and guidance. David Belitz, president of the family office, was also the managing partner of the Chattanooga Renaissance Fund (CRF), our "brother" local angel fund and became a trusted mentor and guide. He generously shared CRF's formation documents and walked our group through the basics of fund formation and structure. David was our hero and I will always be indebted to him for his guidance and patience in answering questions from the beginning days to now.

Our Collective Superpower

I could never have launched an angel investment fund without the expertise and support of my managing partners—a psychologist, a bank executive, a trust officer, two serial entrepreneurs, and a human resources strategist. Each brought not only a wealth of knowledge and business acumen, they also opened their rolodexes and worked diligently to recruit other women to invest in our first fund. They also each came with their own "superpower" that added huge value to our work as we navigated a new world of making early stage investments in female founders. Empathy, optimism, learning, social networking, coaching, trust and discernment all became central tenets of our team because of what each of these dynamic women brought to the table.

The following profiles my seven partners through personal interviews, each offering her own unique story about how and why she jumped into building and leading Jump-Fund. Our work together over the past ten years has taken immense time, energy, headspace, and all of our many and varied talents to be successful. At the core, is a group of women who came together through a shared vision and belief that we could make a difference and change the narrative for other women. We have been humbled in this work, but also very proud of what we have accomplished and eager to share our learnings with others who will pick up the mantle and continue to pay it forward. I hope you will be inspired by their individual stories and the unique superpowers they bring to JumpFund's collective mission and vision.

Shelley: Leading Like a Girl

For Shelley, entrepreneurial education should begin at an early age. In her mind, that education has to include building confidence in girls to lead and start their own businesses. "In the next few years over 60% of college graduates will be women," notes Shelley, "so we need to encourage more girls to demand a seat at the table and have the confidence to do what it takes to get there." In 2015, Shelley presented at TedxBarcelona with a talk titled "Lead Like a Girl." In the presentation, she calls for women to embrace their nurturing, compassionate, sharing and caring selves and couple that with "badass" leadership that is both results-driven and community building. In her TEDx talk she states "feeling deeply is my superpower—I am an empathic badass."

Having come from the world of psychology and counseling, which is female dominated, Shelley's colleagues had always been women. In 2010, Shelley was working as a licensed psychologist with the Center for Integrative Medicine in Chattanooga, when she was recruited as Director of Happiness (her chosen title) for a local startup incubator, the Lamp Post Group (LPG). LPG was led by four male partners and worked with all-male startup teams which was a new and somewhat shocking work environment for Shelley. "It was kind of turned upside down and I didn't get it," she says. "I think honestly, part of me felt so alone. There's me and one (female) designer, no other women in that space at all."

In her role as Director of Happiness, Shelley served as coach, cheerleader, social worker, and mental health support for the startup teams as well as the managing partners. LPG had been launched by the co-founders of Access America, a successful logistics startup run by three partners, who grew their company to hundreds of millions in value and sold to Coyote Logistics in 2015. One of the first venture capital programs of its kind in Chattanooga, it used a "reverse incubator" model wherein the firm took a large ownership stake and provided early funding for the selected startups. As the companies ideally grew and experienced success, they could "buy back" their equity and fly the LPG nest to grow on their own. As part of the Lamp Post family, startup founders could expect "to join a thriving community of entrepreneurs and mentors tackling the same challenges" and access back office support such as human resources, accounting, and finance.

As founders themselves, the LPG partners knew the mental and emotional toll the startup grind entailed. According to one of the LPG partners they needed Shelley because "entrepreneurs are batshit crazy and we need a shrink on site." In those early days, Shelley understood the pain and frustration of being the only woman in this male-dominated incubator. "I felt like I had been given this opportunity at Lamp Post and was invited in because I was psychologically-minded, but then felt like I had to fight my way to the table, which made me feel responsible to open up doors for other women."

For Shelley, her "aha!" moment was in 2012 at the first GigTank, a pitch competition for companies drawn to Chattanooga's early, high-speed internet. As mentioned previously, the early GigTank showdowns featured all-male-led companies and Shelley was witnessing the same disparities at LPG. Shelley recalls talking to the LPG partners about this and why they weren't investing in any women-led companies. The response was that their door was always open to female founders, but they were not seeing many apply for support.

Around this same time, Shelley was introduced to Tiffanie Robinson, a serial entrepreneur who was head of marketing for RiverCity Company, a downtown development organization. Finding Tiffanie equally passionate about the inequity they witnessed in Chattanooga's burgeoning startup ecosystem, they decided to bring together smart women and get them talking. Shelley remembers the very first gathering of women in a conference room at LPG: "There were probably twenty-five women and I remember one of the Lamp Post partners looked in and was like, 'holy shit. Look at all these powerhouse women. What are *they* doing in our office?"

At Lamp Post, Shelley was learning about tech and finance and how the system is built. As she delved deeper, she felt even more mission-driven to figure out what to do to change this inequitable system. According to Shelley, "We needed to figure out how to deconstruct and disrupt. That's what I think sustained me and still does to this day. That's the bigger piece of this that I still get fired up about. There was a point where I knew we couldn't really do anything impactful without money."

When it became clear to our group that raising capital of our own was the answer, Shelley felt totally out of her league. She remembers feeling like she had no idea how to do it, but that it felt totally right, because it is exactly the problem women leading startups face. "I was not conditioned to really think about money, or how money is the linchpin for these power structures that feel so out of balance," mused Shelley, "I knew that if we were going to sit at the table and have any kind of power in these conversations we had to raise money."

Being a relational person, and interested in people's emotional intelligence, Shelley feels JumpFund's success has been in large part a testament to the supportive relationship of our founding team. According to Shelley, there is something unique about our group, when most of the time you get a "bunch of women like us and it's pretty competitive." Instead, she feels like "we're women supporting women—I have never felt competitive with our team, it was always outside of our group that I felt like I had to prove myself," relates Shelley. She has a feeling of "coming home" with JumpFund partners that she had not found elsewhere in her career.

Our relationship as a general partner group and teamwork has always been founded on open communication. According to Shelley, we didn't let things fester and become a conflict. From the beginning, she felt our group was self aware and very cognizant of ego. The sisterhood we had developed, supporting each other and working together through highs and lows, and recognizing each other's strengths and weaknesses helped her through challenging times as she navigated building and ultimately winding up her own tech startup. She remembers thinking, "I don't have to be anything other than who I am and show up for this group of women. That's really rare."

Ten years after founding JumpFund, Shelley feels that our work has helped change the lens through which investments are made in Chattanooga and beyond. Yet, she looks forward to the day when we will no longer need women-focused funds. She continues to have conversations with men starting funds or incubators who will talk to her about recruiting women. Her fear is that without JumpFund's presence and our active investment, it's going to be easier for male funders to de-value gender parity or female leadership. Her hope is that through JumpFund's investment in other women, these badass, empathetic leaders will continue to pay it forward and invest in more women.

Tiffanie: The Optimist

The year we started the fund, our partners all participated in Golden Seeds' Angel Investor 101 course in New York City during their annual summit in January. We have always been extremely frugal as a management team and thus were crammed in, four to a room, sharing beds and bathrooms for a few days. It was a cold, snowy day and we worried we might get stuck in New York given the weather, which especially worried Tiffanie who was a new mother at the time (her first of three boys). I remember Tiffanie sitting on the floor doing her makeup that morning in front of the bedroom mirror, as someone else was occupying the bathroom. We were all chatting and giddy about what we were learning and the huge potential of what we were launching with JumpFund. At that moment, Tiffanie turned and said, "We could make a shit ton of money doing this!" With all of the newness and riskiness launching a fund entailed, her optimism was needed and infectious for our group. Yes, we could make money doing this work and that was okay to talk about.

Tiffanie has always been the "young gun"of our group, almost 15 years my junior, with an ambition and drive that puts us all to shame. With a career as a serial entrepreneur, Tiffanie has launched several businesses including a local eatery called Fork & Pie and WayPaver, an HR firm for innovative tech and startup talent. Currently, she is CEO of her own multi-million dollar commercial real estate business, in her second term and now chair of our county school board, and mother of three young, active boys, in addition to her role as a partner at JumpFund. I frankly don't know when she has time to sleep.

When we started JumpFund, Tiffanie was working with River City Company, our public/private downtown development agency, where she was Director of Creative Strategy. At River City, Tiffanie had developed a pop-up business revitalization program in our downtown core, both to activate the city streets as well as allow entrepreneurs to pilot their businesses with real customers. Her passion for entrepreneurship runs deep, and she recognized early the opportunity gap for women, especially those like her with the drive and determination to start their own business.

When Tiffanie gets a fire in her belly about something you don't want to mess with her. She addressed the plight of women entrepreneurs with optimism and, as she says, the "blind naivete" of youth. "In our restaurant and catering businesses, I was truly a co-owner (with husband Mike)," says Tiffanie, "and this made me think about why are there not more female entrepreneurs starting businesses." The deeper she looked into the issue, she realized it was because women didn't feel like they had a platform to jump off from, or support from others, that would make that first leap easier.

Tiffanie and Shelley were the first of our group to bring together local women to discuss the lack of gender diversity in our entrepreneurial ecosystem, which was the spark that led to launching JumpFund. At her first lunch meeting with Shelley, Tiffanie remembers telling her that if she could do anything she wanted, it would be to start a fund made up of women for women. Tiffanie recalls thinking she'd like to accomplish that later in life, maybe in twenty years when she was more fully established in her career. But she remembers Shelley saying, "Why would any of us wait for that? We need that now."

As JumpFund launched, Tiffanie felt like she had found her tribe and has been dedicated ever since to uplifting women entrepreneurs. "I think I've brought optimism to the table and the entrepreneurs viewpoint," says Tiffanie. She is proud that through JumpFund, she has helped other women in the Southeast make their ventures a reality, and believes strongly that without us, many would not have received the capital they needed to grow. She believes that JumpFund's secondary role as a cheerleader and advisor for many of our portfolio companies has also been a game-changer for these women leaders. "We've been involved in scenarios where we helped get an entrepreneur out of a difficult, abusive situation," says Tiffanie. "It is hard to be a female CEO trying to make something change in the boardroom when no one else around the table is a woman."

Tiffanie has experienced being the lone woman at the executive table repeatedly in her career. She remembers in particular her first maternity leave as CEO of LampPost Properties, the real estate arm of the LampPost Group, which develops downtown housing and collaborative office spaces. "They (the board) never asked me what I needed as a CEO, like how much time do you think that you need to go on maternity leave and feel like you can return with the right amount of energy to lead your company?" She believes women leaders would ask those questions, putting themselves in the shoes of the entrepreneur juggling work/life balance. Women would be more likely to ask, "How are you doing? How can we support you?"

Women corporate leaders have become more vocal in recent years about expanding family leave policies and support for working women to succeed. The pandemic which set women back financially due to their dual roles as parents and employees working both jobs from home has brought these issues even more to light. Some companies are beginning to respond with more flexible work opportunities, dual parent leave, and support for childcare, but the American economy has a long way to go in addressing the needs of working women. As a woman in business, often the only one in the boardroom or C-suite, Tiffanie has appreciated the supportive tribe we have built as partners of JumpFund. "For years there were times in my professional life where it was difficult to go to work every day, but JumpFund was a bright spot for me," says Tiffanie, "I was able to learn so much from every single one of you."

She cautions others starting their own funds to think critically about who they bring together to manage the fund or serve on an investment committee. Pulling in a diversity of skill sets to support the growth and development of a fund is of utmost importance, as it is with any nascent business. "I think we did a good job of putting people together that think differently and have (a variety of) skill sets," Tiffanie observes, "it's natural and easy to just automatically pull people together that think like you, but I would challenge people to get out of their own way and go find partners that think differently." Akin to the diversity of opinions we applaud in our startups, she understands that discourse and robust dialogue are important in fund management.

Yet, she is crystal clear that our work is far from being done. While she does feel the needle has moved, especially with the growth of entities such as JumpFund and the rise of women leaders harnessing their capital to make an impact, she thinks it will be another generation or more until we can see real parity. She is concerned about the reversal of public policies affecting women in the workforce, setting us back even further, especially as revealed by the pandemic. "You're seeing women's rights being taken away, left and right," she says, "there's absolutely no way that it doesn't impact the boardroom, both in the public and private sector. So I think that unfortunately, our work is more important now than ever."

As the mother of three boys, she is committed to raising her children to see themselves as equal partners with women, in every aspect of their lives. She recommends the book *Raising Boys to Respect Girls*, by Dave Willis, which speaks to the pervasive nature of sexism and inequality facing women in our society. According to Tiffanie, "until women can truly go to work, have a career, and not feel like they are still carrying the full burden of their household with them every day, I'm not sure that there will be equity within the entrepreneurial space for women." We look forward to watching Tiffanie's boys grow into avid feminists who value parity and respect strong, courageous women like their mother as partners in business and life.

Stefanie: The Social Capitalist

With a thirty-year career in banking, Stefanie has stories to tell. Banking and finance is still a male-dominated industry and Stefanie worked diligently to climb up the ranks, only to hit a glass ceiling at the pinnacle of her career. She now runs her own financial advisory firm, Aegle Wealth, after years of pounding her head against the wall of traditional finance and discovering another path on her journey with JumpFund.

Starting at Bank of America in the 1990's, Stefanie managed high net worth clients, who were mostly male, and realized early on that women were not being invited to the table to participate in personal financial decisions for their families. Stefanie felt that the men in her industry did not believe their female clients wanted to spend their time talking about their finances. According to Stefanie, their attitude was: "trust us because we are the experts and we can give good advice and don't want to overwhelm them."

Fast forward several years and Stefanie had the opportunity to join a "de novo" or startup bank emerging in Chattanooga. Jumping into this yet unproven bank felt risky as they were starting from the ground up. But she knew it would be exciting to be part of building an organization and found the new bank's thesis exciting and attractive: helping serve entrepreneurs in our local community and establishing a more approachable, non-corporate bank. As Executive Vice President of Investor Relations, Stefanie was part of the bank's founding team, but did not ultimately have a seat at the decision-making table. This frustrated her as she had worked her way up the corporate banking ladder and had what it took to be a chief executive, especially as they were growing their nascent business. In fact, most of the investors she worked with as well as board members assumed she was at the C-Level. When our group of women initiated conversations with her about starting JumpFund, Stefanie saw it as a way to pay it forward for other women to create their own C suites. For Stefanie, JumpFund was an opportunity to hand the ball to women who could be in charge of their own board-rooms.

Stefanie was hugely instrumental in helping attract JumpFund investors and raise funds. With a rolodex of high net worth women, especially those she felt had gone untapped by her male colleagues, she found women eager for the chance to direct their capital to something purposeful and mission-driven but also focused on returns. Stefanie recalls how the social and professional network she had built throughout her career really paid off. "By virtue of my network, there were women that were walking into the bank to talk to me about the Jumpfund," says Stefanie.

Stefanie points to her community engagement outside of the bank—in leadership positions and on the boards of several nonprofit organizations throughout her career, from our local women's fund and women's leadership institute to the United Way and a regional nature center—as a key to bringing like-minded investors to JumpFund. She discovered that although her banking relationships were majority male, her nonprofit relationships were 99% female. She realized there was an opportunity to pitch JumpFund to the women she worked with in the philanthropic community as a way to both do good and make a return on their investment. "I had these two worlds," says Stefanie. "One was my financial world, where I was making money, but which was male-dominated, and had a certain ideology. And then I had my community involvement world, where I was also in leadership, with a bunch of women running things, but not making money." Stefanie thought, what if we channeled this population? To Stefanie, it was a "call to action" for women leaders to engage with their money for good, leaning into female empowerment and paying it forward.

An alternative pitch to investors came from a longtime

(male) advisor of hers, who appreciated what JumpFund was building, and later became an investor himself. He saw the JumpFund opportunity not as just a feel good, "social movement" but one of arbitrage, an investment opportunity that only we were able to deliver on. Stefanie remembers her conversation with this advisor:

> *"He told me to sell this as an investment opportunity. If stellar women who are accomplished in their fields, who have business training, aren't getting capital and subsequently are often discounted and men are trading at a premium, what kind of arbitrage opportunity might that present? That's a financial concept that pretty much anybody can understand—if I can buy this on discount and get equal or superior returns, that's a great investment."*

As it turns out, this second pitch resonated even more deeply with JumpFund investors, as it spoke to both the inequities in the market as well as the opportunity for an outsized return. And although we focused only on female investors in our first fund, proving the point that there *were* women who would invest in this asset class, there were also many male investors for whom this line of reasoning began to peak their interest. In our second fund, with an established track record, we were able to use the arbitrage pitch to our advantage and recruit what we like to call "a few good men" to diversify our investor pool.

Stefanie was also the first one to suggest pulling together a group of investors who might not be able to commit $30,000 a share individually to the first fund, but wanted to join our effort. She created Cannonball LLC (pun intended), a special purpose vehicle (SPV), to gather these investors and harness their capital which spawned SPVs led by other partners. Through her efforts and cheerleading, we were able to attract even more women to the table and expand our limited partner network of expertise and social capital for our entrepreneurs.

With fundraising, Stefanie is clear that women should never underestimate the power of social capital. She felt JumpFund's superpower was the fact that our founding team had built strong networks of women in leadership. "As a group we had very complementary networks," recalls Stefanie, "so it took us no time to have people coming in our door."

According to Stefanie, if you said social capital was an asset in a banking environment, they would laugh you out the door. But in the angel space, social capital is highly prized. In addition to recruiting investors, JumpFund's connections also helped with access to high quality deals. The community of women investing in women of which we are now an integral part, Stefanie says, "has allowed us to play at a high level, even though we are a fairly small fund. People don't think of us as a less than $10 million operation."

For Stefanie, JumpFund has been about finding her tribe. After spending her career in banking and the male-dominated field of finance, it has been refreshing to be at financial decision-making tables with all women. The Jump-Fund was Stefanie's first real opportunity twenty years into her career where she could observe and take part in how a female majority makes decisions and how women assess risk. "When we talk about gender differences, I feel like I've lived it with JumpFund," says Stefanie," I could say things in JumpFund world that were not discounted or discredited." Stefanie finds that in the banking world, nobody wants to talk about your gut feelings, your intuition. They focus on numbers, facts, and data, which are all part of the conversation in JumpFund, but, Stefanie says, "we also lean into our fundamental impressions, feelings, and nuances to assess a potential investment."

In the end, being an integral part of JumpFund propelled

Stefanie to leave her 30 year career in banking and start her own venture, Aegle Wealth. Having spent her career working around "successful southern Boomer banking management executives" who she feels saw only one way to approach finance, JumpFund supported her burgeoning belief that there were alternatives to the traditional financial structures and attitudes. For Stefanie, JumpFund was her first chance to put her money where her mouth was. "It's one thing to talk about it but it's another to put in your energy and your own capital," says Stefanie. And because of JumpFund, people now seek her out as their financial advisor. They know she is committed to diversity and equity, women's empowerment and democratizing finance.

To those looking to launch their own funds, Stefanie offers a word of caution. She suggests that those interested in early stage investing begin by joining a network of like-minded investors, committing smaller dollar amounts out of the gate. She herself has recently engaged with her alma mater Notre Dame's Irish Angels, one of many alumni angel networks. She also suggests you study a wide variety of groups to understand their operations, communications and deal making. Or, form your own limited partnership or SPV as she did with Cannonball, LLC, and get into a few deals alongside some angel groups for which you share an affinity, which she says, "is a great way to have an entree without the mammoth responsibility of a fund."

The future looks bright to Stefanie, in part due to the multiplier effect of JumpFund and many others like us who have begun to change the conversation in finance, who want our capital to have more impact, and who want women to have a seat at the table or better yet, create their own corporate tables that are diverse and unbiased. She feels that JumpFund's legacy is having helped nurture a thriving ecosystem of women investing in women. In her own practice, Stefanie continues to support women who own and operate small businesses, helping them make key decisions about managing their wealth and their companies. The social network she has built and engaged with through JumpFund continues to grow and support many more women as they activate their capital and pay it forward for the next generation of female entrepreneurs.

Betsy: Officer of Trust

As a seasoned trust officer in a fiduciary role, Betsy understands that her greatest power is that of discernment, her ability to sit back and listen, weighing the pros and cons of a pitch with the insight that comes from decades in finance. Beginning her career in the wealth management sector at big banks and graduating to work with families and their wealth transitions in the trust industry, Betsy is a keen listener and avid proponent of the power of storytelling and legacy creation. Now CEO of her own trust company, Pendelton Square Trust, Betsy has spent her career working with women of means—wealth often left to them by their spouses—who have had no exposure to angel investing.

Betsy was drawn to the mission and vision of JumpFund early on and has added tremendous value with her background in finance as well as her ability to ask discerning, astute questions of entrepreneurs. She was excited to join a group of like-minded women who were jumping into this asset class and she frankly felt she would have FOMO (fear of missing out) if she didn't come onboard at our early stage. She immediately understood that the world of angel investing and working with early stage companies was nothing akin to the traditional world of banking, as there were often no real financials to analyze (only hypotheses and predictions) and little to base future performance on except the confidence in the entrepreneur to execute on her vision. She quickly found that this work involved much more heart, feeling, and psychology as well as establishing strong relationships with founders to support them through all of the ups and downs.

Betsy remembers the first due diligence checklist we received back from an entrepreneur, with fifty or more items we had requested—from marketing plans to financial projections—and only ten items they could supply. She was used to seeing cash flow analyses and many companies who pitched us barely had any revenue. "I learned pretty early on at JumpFund," recalls Betsy, "that beyond the business basics, there's not a lot of logic and numbers analysis that goes into making the final investment decision … it's really about the person and the idea, their passion and execution." Betsy came to understand that angel investing is more about relationships and confidence in the people in whom you're investing than spreadsheets.

Betsy's excitement for JumpFund's mission was also about educating more women about this asset class and the opportunity to invest in other women. In both her banking and trust company roles, Betsy had worked with many women leaders who were "social patrons" in philanthropy and saw an opportunity to attract these same women to the cause of increasing access to capital for female founders. "I worked with many women who really didn't have the interest or time to devote to learning about capital markets, and really didn't understand the components of investing," says Betsy, "I thought: if they knew the founder of the company, and it was an industry they were interested in, this could be a great educational tool to learn about investments and teach them the components of angel investing."

As a partner in JumpFund, Betsy was inspired by other women taking the bold leap to start their own ventures, and decided to launch her own trust company in 2015, capitalizing on Tennessee's favorable trust laws. After a few years co-leading the venture, which has grown to over \$2B AUM (assets under management), Betsy stepped in as CEO and took the reins of their twenty-person team. She now understands the many pain points of entrepreneurship, as she worked to raise capital for her own business in a tightly regulated market and has managed everything from sales and new client acquisition to human resources and board relations.

In her heart, she understands that it is the passion for your work that drives you forward combined with continuous learning and a growth mindset. "I like to say I kind of did this backwards," says Betsy, "because I jumped into the angel investing world before I was an entrepreneur." But her road to CEO was inspired through her experiences of meeting and investing in female entrepreneurs as well as "our tight knit group of fearless women," which gave her the confidence to do something more risky in her career.

Her advice to others stepping into angel investing and potentially building their own funds or angel network is threefold. First, have patience and stamina, as startup investing has a long time horizon and many ups and downs. Second, Betsy sees that part of JumpFund's success has been our active engagement in growing the field of gender lens investing and building a network of other funding partners committed to this work. "You can't just sit and wait for these companies to come to you," opines Betsy. "Some of our best deals and investments have come through relationships with other angel funds with which we've co-invested." And finally, Betsy recommends that finding companies you can be passionate about and engage with "beyond the check" long-term to provide resources, advice, and mentorship has been a key factor in our continued success.

Betsy feels that to reach gender parity in entrepreneurship it will be important that funds like ours share the stories of these successes and change the perception around the capabilities of women as business leaders. It is important that we rewrite the narrative around why diverse teams are essential to long term business success and growth. Betsy is hoping that many of the high-flyers in our portfolios will do just that and we will shout their success from the rooftops.

Cory: Lifelong Learner

Cory is an eager, self-described lifelong learner who engages her heart and soul in everything she does. As the daughter of Korean immigrants who grew up in Baltimore, Maryland, working every day at her family's small grocery, she learned early the importance of grit, determination, and self-preservation. As a first generation college student, she was eager to gain new knowledge and take on any challenge that came her way. But she admits that she had a blind spot for the struggles of women and minorities, especially in business, as she felt that she had successfully forged her own path despite the biases against her as an Asian woman in tech.

Early in her career, Cory worked in data warehousing for Provident disability insurance (now Unum) and later at Krystal, a southern fast food franchise, both headquartered in Chattanooga. "I literally was the only girl in the IT department," recalls Cory. There, she remembers the older guys saying, 'You think you're cool, because you have an MBA and you're decades younger than us.' I was not in the club, they made it clear."

Although she has spent most of her career in male dominant fields, she never thought of herself as a minority. "I just walk in there and go find my place and if it doesn't look like it's a good place for me, I walk away," says Cory, "not worrying about if I do not fit in because of color or sex, it really never occurred to me." So, when she learned that female founders are not funded at anywhere near the same rate as men, it piqued her interest and made her want to learn more about the bias and the underlying prejudices.

Addressing bias and connecting with other women entrepreneurs has been Cory's main passion working with JumpFund. Since joining JumpFund as a general partner, Cory has launched two of her own ventures, one in technology and the other in healthcare, both fields in which she has deep experience. She has enjoyed sharing her journey with other female founders as she empathizes with their struggles and has experienced the hard work and daily grind it takes to run a business.

Cory acknowledges that throughout her career she has experienced bias, but didn't let it stop her from pursuing her work, even if at times it made things more difficult or uncomfortable. Her personal mantra has been, "How do I make this place work for me." Growing up attending Baltimore City Schools, as one of the only Asian students at the time, she says, "I think I learned quickly, don't worry about it. You're a human being, and you just go do whatever you need to do." Later, at an all girls school she began to feel more empowered that she could do whatever she wanted in life. Eventually, she would pursue an MBA and witnessed other impressive women becoming business leaders who were "fighters" just like her.

She also understands the highs and lows of entrepreneurship as she has had her share of both triumphs and failures. "My own personal experience really made me softer for the heart of the entrepreneur," says Cory. One of JumpFund entrepreneurs Cory worked most closely with was Lucy Beard, CEO of one of our early rising star companies, Feetz which 3D-printed customizable shoes. Feetz attracted venture capital from a large West Coast

VC firm, which later had an adverse impact on the young company and drove Lucy out, and eventually the technology was sold to a new shoe brand. It was a hard road for Lucy and she had many regrets, one of which was taking funding from what turned out to be an abusive and malicious funding source. Cory counseled Lucy through all of it, telling her "move on girl, you're fine, don't lose sleep over it. We're proud of you, no matter what."

A serial entrepreneur, Cory is now CEO of KelCor, a medical device company bringing a new kind of sterile taping system to hospitals. As she launches one of her latest companies and re-experiences all the joys and pains of early stage startups, she leans into her personal journey as a life-long learner and takes the highs and lows in stride. She understands that both in her work as an entrepreneur and partner in JumpFund, this work is a marathon, not a sprint. She is proud to have been a part of our effort to elevate the conversation about gender equity in the Southeast startup ecosystem and is hopeful that new generations of investors will better understand the importance of supporting diverse teams and women's leadership. According to Cory, "It's about the team and who are the people that are going to make the next great products."

Kim: The Company Coach

Kim and I met around a conference room table of other women new to angel investing at our first Golden Seeds Summit in January 2014 in New York City. As two of the only women in the Angel Investing 101 program who were not native Northeasterners nor finance professionals, we naturally gravitated towards each other. Later that night at a private dinner in the Park Avenue apartment of one of Golden Seeds' founding partners, we started talking about how Kim, who lives in Atlanta, had been introduced to Golden Seeds through one of her colleagues at Mercer, a large Human Resources consulting firm. I told Kim about our newly launched JumpFund in Chattanooga (just up the road from Atlanta) and that we were attending Golden Seeds' training to become immersed in this asset class and learn from others on the forefront of gender lens investing.

Kim had become intrigued with the opportunity to directly invest in women through Mercer's involvement in the World Economic Forum, which was focused on how to help women thrive. Specifically, Mercer had analyzed the economic imperative of keeping women in the workforce towards the goal of equal rates of women's economic participation and the impact that could have on global GDP (gross domestic product). Through this work, Kim and Pam Jeffords, her sister and Mercer colleague, were witnessing an exodus of women leaving corporate America to go start their own companies. The two were interested in how to find those women and help support and amplify them as they built and grew their businesses. Kim remembers thinking, "I need to put my money where my mouth is, I need to invest in women." So, she joined Golden Seeds as a first step to becoming an angel investor and access their robust deal flow of women-led ventures.

After our first meeting in New York, Kim decided to invest in JumpFund as another way to more quickly diversify her personal portfolio and support women-led companies specifically in the Southeast. "What I liked about JumpFund was the opportunity to put my capital to use in a more scalable way versus me finding every individual company and doing all that diligence," recalls Kim, "and it would also help diversify some of my risk."

Meanwhile, Kim was beginning to dive more seriously into angel investing and even co-founded an Atlanta Golden Seeds chapter (one of the largest networks of angel investing in women in the U.S.). As her passion for working with early stage entrepreneurs grew, she began to feel the pull to do something different with her career and eventually left Mercer to pursue angel investing and coaching female founders full-time. Besides holding monthly office hours in Atlanta for Golden Seeds, Kim became involved as an advisor for former Atlanta Mayor Kasim Reed's new Women's Entrepreneurship Initiative (WEI) which was launched "to provide unprecedented access to the human, educational, and financial capital critical to empowering early stage company-building entrepreneurs, who just so happen to be women."[4]

As an increasingly active and valuable limited partner in JumpFund, we turned to Kim as we began to consider launching a second fund and asked her to join our general partner team. One of the reasons we asked Kim to join JumpFund II was her full-time engagement in this work and dedication to supporting women entrepreneurs. At the time we launched JumpFund II, my other partners were dedicating more time to their own growing ventures and Kim became another partner with whom to share the load of running a fund. She also serves as a direct connection to the active Atlanta venture market in which much of our deal flow and eventually several portfolio companies are headquartered.

Kim's favorite part of this work is directly engaging with companies, and feels her "superpower" in our group and as an angel investor is "influencing people to reach their full potential." According to Kim, she feels like her background in HR and working with a wide variety of company leaders has positioned her well to encourage others to stretch themselves to reach their goals. The number one question she gets asked is, *How did an HR person end up as an angel investor?* But to Kim, her transition from HR executive to startup investing makes a lot of sense. Her experience brings a different lens to our portfolio companies in terms of people and talent strategy.

"It's a lot of fun to work with these startups," says Kim. "I feel like I do a good job of motivating people to do what they need to do to be successful, to keep going when things are tough." Kim also enjoys judging pitch competitions and sitting on investor panels to bring a different perspective from the traditional finance industry. Says Kim, "I love hearing why people were inspired to start their companies, what problem they are solving and why they are passionate about solving that problem."

Kim has brought several Atlanta-based companies into JumpFund portfolio and works closely with many of them, coaching and consulting as they grow. She met founder Jenn Graham of Civic Dinners at a very early stage when Jenn was first going through Mayor Reed's WEI program. Jenn originally started Civic Dinners with an eye to serving local government by facilitating community-wide conversations on a variety of topics, from transportation to environmental issues. As her WEI program mentor, Kim encouraged Jenn to think bigger and develop her "dinners" into a technology-based platform that could serve large enterprises grappling with employee engagement. "We decided there was a growth venture in Civic Dinners," remembers Kim. "That the problem she was solving was not for the individual as much as it was a tool for enterprise. Getting her to make that pivot was huge and it was a lot of work on my part just getting her to see her potential."

It was not until after Jenn had completed Engage, a corporate accelerator program designed for companies looking to "engage" with many of Atlanta's largest corporations as customers—Delta, Home Depot, Coca Cola—that Civic Dinners became a growth venture suitable for outside investors such as JumpFund. After raising its first outside capital, the company rebranded to Inclusivv in 2020, pivoting solely to an online platform during the pandemic, and inked six figure contracts with corporations such as Facebook, Coca Cola, and Mailchimp. Inclusivv now tackles tough, curated conversations like Women and Work, Allyship, and Bridging the Racial Divide and is being used by large enterprises to expand Diversity, Equity and Inclusion (DEI) initiatives.

In addition to company coaching, Kim was an essential partner in our fundraising efforts for our second fund as we toured the Southeast. We even journeyed to Colorado, where Kim's sister pulled together a group that eventually invested, to share our story and meet with other women intrigued with angel investing but not knowing where to start. Our "roadshow" as Kim calls it, involved a mini-Angel investing 101 session to help educate more women about this asset class and how they could incorporate it into their broader investment portfolio strategy. "I really enjoyed those meetings," recalls Kim, "explaining what it was to actually invest in startups and educating a whole new group of investors who would not normally have been writing checks." These small group meetings were more comfortable for women so they wouldn't feel like they were asking "stupid" questions about what it means to be an angel investor or a limited partner in a fund. Kim even remembers one woman just wanted to give us a check for fifty grand right then and there, to which she replied, "well thank you, but that's not how this works" as venture funds typically call capital over a period of time as investment opportunities arise.

A staunch advocate of growing women as business leaders, Kim feels it is also important for women who have been successful to "get in there and write checks." But what keeps women from jumping into angel investing? Kim believes that women process and analyze things differently, we need more facts, information and some guarantee that we'll be successful before we go do something. For that reason, it takes women doing their homework and gaining knowledge to be ready to take the leap. Kim's hope is that examples from funds engaged in gender lens investing, such as JumpFund, will help more women feel comfortable "jumping in" and paying it forward.

Invest in Your Team

It is well known in angel investing circles that startup success is 90% about the team and leadership of the company. The JumpFund's success has clearly been because of this amazing group of women, each with their own expertise, knowledge, and superpower that has added value to our work. As a group of women that was wholly new to angel investing we have done well for our first rodeo—whether it has been our success at working directly with entrepreneurs, building a network of like-minded investors, or picking the "right" companies in which to invest. I would advise anyone stepping into this journey, whether you are joining or forming a group with which to invest, to think carefully about who you want on your team and what will make it most successful. While it has not all been roses, we have leaned into our strengths and championed each other as we have all taken on new challenges, being respectful and humble along the way. As we say to our entrepreneurs, this is a marriage and we need to find ways to work together through thick and thin.

One of the best things we did as a group was to have Shelley help us identify our Enneagram types. The Enneagram has made a resurgence in business leadership circles and in self-help seminars as a tool for growth and self-discovery. On the surface, it is similar to a personality test you might take from a human resource perspective, identifying your strengths and weaknesses and how you see the world and solve problems. Yet the Enneagram has much deeper complexity as you study its nuances and can tell you much about how you interact with others and respond to stress in your life. By exploring our own Enneagram archetypes and how we interact with other "types" it helped build more trust and understanding among our group of high powered, hard charging women. While several of us tested as Enneagram number Threes (Achievers) or Ones (Perfectionists) on the Enneagram spectrum, several of us were also Twos (Helpers) or even Eights (Challengers), all perspectives which lend depth and complexity to our relationships and how we also serve our portfolio companies.

Another activity we did together before starting our second fund, was to take a retreat to regroup on our mission and vision. Generally, funds have a minimum ten-year life cycle with two one-year extensions, depending on the life cycles of the portfolio companies, so each new fund is a long-term endeavor and not one to take lightly. It was important that this founding group of women was either all in or not as we took steps to build a second portfolio of companies and had to tap back into our networks to fundraise. We had learned a lot in our first round and certainly wanted to stay in and further invest in several of our companies that were doing well and had the markers for continued successful growth and potentially strong exits.

So, we gathered together for a weekend in the mountains of North Carolina in the Spring of 2016 to decide our next fund's destiny. Most funds have at least two or more "vintages" and many are run by career venture capitalists who continue to build additional fund vehicles for investing long-term. We were a group of women new to this asset class, who had been learning much about early stage investing and felt good about our first portfolio of companies, but were still trying to assess whether this was a good investment of our own time, talents and resources.

JumpFund I had been a grand experiment and we were extremely proud of what we had accomplished, proving that both the pipeline of quality, high growth, women-led companies existed in the Southeast as well as women's capital to support them.

After hiking, eating and laughing together, all good medicine for any group working together, we sat in the living room by the fire to dive deeper into each of our hopes, fears, and intentions about launching a second fund. As managing partner and the one who was investing my full time and energy into this endeavor, I wanted to be able to continue this work, doubling down on the success we were seeing and raising new capital to invest in more women-led ventures. As managing partners, I had a taste of what this could be and wanted us to be able to do more. My partners were not as sure. They knew how much work it would take, especially with fundraising, and the timeline of each fund which seemed daunting (another ten or more years working together?).

As part of our process, we brainstormed all of the words we associated with JumpFund after our almost four years (at that time) working together. A "word cloud" came out of that session, one I still have in my office today. It was filled with inspirational words such as change-agent, badass, conscious capitalism, empowerment, and my favorite, "girlband," as well as cautionary missives like love/hate, risky and scary. We knew we would need to be all-in on a second fund and thankfully, after our weekend together and diving into what was really driving us to do this work, we decided to jump back in.

Jumping In, Again

Raising the second fund was not as easy as our first. We had proven the initial concept and had one successful exit under our belt. Yet, it was an uphill battle convincing our current investors to double down on their investment in us. Talking to other women general partners, this is a somewhat common refrain with women angel investors. They are not as likely to see the advantages of investing more money as "follow-on" capital to their initial investment, growing its potential, when they haven't seen the full returns. Unfortunately, this is akin to folding your cards after the first round or two of poker, the risk is seen as too great. In some cases, many of our investors just did not have the cash on hand at the time to make a second investment as we were launching our fund in 2017 and some were still reeling from the latest financial crisis.

Thus, our second fundraise was a bit more of a slog and took us over a year when our first raise took less than six months. Albeit, we were raising twice as much money and the stakes were higher as we had an active portfolio of companies we wanted to continue to support and grow. What we did find though was that due to our networking with other gender lens investors and getting our name out beyond the Southeast, we had more credibility with new investors who were looking for ways to invest in women-led ventures. We even attracted what we like to call "a few good men" who had heard our pitch and wanted to diversify their own portfolios with women's leadership. Bringing in Kim Seals as a new general partner, who had been an investor in our first fund, also added to our exposure to new investors with her network in Atlanta and even Colorado.

Now, more than five years into our second fund, we believe our time and energy is best spent on our portfolio of amazing woman-led ventures and shepherding these companies to successful exits rather than launching a new fund. This work takes stamina and committed leadership, as well as raising significantly more capital, all of which none of us had the interest in pursuing a third time around. Today, we are nearing the ten year anniversary of our first fund and at mid-stride into our second fund. We have had a few wins and many losses, with several of our most successful portfolio companies experiencing significant gains, which we are banking on to ultimately bring strong returns for our investors. Our goal now is to prove that investing through a gender lens produces strong returns both for our investors as well as the women in which we invest.

We are not career venture capitalists, but instead a group of badass women who saw a big problem and leaned into offering our own solution. The aha moment of ten years ago has blossomed into a movement, joined by countless other women across the globe, and we are proud to have been a small part of the rising tide of women investing in women. In Act III, I provide a more detailed "how to" guide for women interested in building their own tribe and collectively investing in women-led ventures. Whether you consider launching a fund, network, or small investment group it is important to first consider who are the right partners to make it a success and who will travel on this journey of learning and growing together. It will make all the difference.

*Word Cloud generated at JumpFund II Planning Retreat, 2017.

ACT III

Flipping the Script

3

Flipping the Script

We will never solve the feminization of power until we solve the masculinity of wealth.

—Gloria Steinem

Gender Lens Investing

When we launched JumpFund we had a myopic view of a much wider, societal problem. As women in business in our own mid-sized city, we saw and had experienced the gender gap in entrepreneurship in our local ecosystem. It was not until at least three years after launching our first fund that we discovered the term "Gender Lens Investing" (GLI) was beginning to be used widely by impact-focused investors. By definition, Gender Lens Investing is an investment approach which aims to advance gender equality by taking into account gender-based factors across the investment process.

In 2017 Suzanne Biegel, held the first ever Gender Lens Investing Summit in the U.S. Self-described Catalyst at Large, Suzanne had successfully re-invested her own capital solely in companies, funds, and initiatives that positively impact women and girls. The GLI Summit was co-sponsored by the Wharton School for Social Impact at the University of Pennsylvania, and JumpFund along with other women-led firms, foundations, and nonprofits gathered to discuss how to further frame and promote this emerging investment strategy. With the rise of women-led venture firms as well as a new wave of Environment, Social, Governance (ESG) impact investment funds considering women's corporate leadership and pay equity, there were now excellent investment opportunities across asset classes with which to support women.

From that first GLI Summit, Biegel and Wharton collaborated on Project Sage, the first comprehensive research study to track and measure the impact of early stage venture firms dedicated to investing with a gender lens. Under Biegel's leadership, the Project Sage report produced four updated versions through 2021, which catalog the rise of women-led venture and private equity firms and other groups investing in women. The reports include any groups identifying as having a "gender mandate" as part of their investment thesis, which can mean: a specific number of investments that must be made with a gender focus and/or a specific amount of capital that must be allocated with a gender focus. The JumpFund has proudly been featured alongside larger, national gender lens investing firms such as Halogen Ventures (CA), Rethink Impact (DC), and Chloe Capital (NY) and we often recommend Project Sage as a resource guide for women entrepreneurs seeking funding.

In their fourth report, Project Sage 4.0, found a 250% increase in GLI firms across the world since the first Project Sage report. This growth represents 206 gender lens funds participating in the survey compared to 58 funds in the original study in 2017. And in 2021 those funds represented a collective $6B in private equity, venture, and early stage funding with a gender lens mandate compared to less than $2B raised only four years previously. More than 60% of the firms were categorized as venture capital while the remaining were defined as private equity or providers of debt capital. And, 68% of these gender lens funds have women in senior leadership while 62% have women on their investment committees.[5]

While this growth is phenomenal and speaks to the

desire of more women actively engaging as investors and leading firms which invest with a gender lens, the total capital raised still speaks to a huge gap in the market. Less than 3% of venture capital goes to women-led companies and according to the IFC (International Finance Corporation) the "capital gap" for women is more than $1.6 Trillion. And many of the GLI funds established in the last few years have raised far less than their initial target investments. Over 60% of the new funds established were "first-time funds" which traditionally face barriers to raising capital without a proven track record of investments in a risky asset class. Layer that with women leading these first-time funds, who face similar bias and discrimination as female founders, and the obstacles to fundraising increase. Added to that, many funds in the study closed their fundraising earlier than planned as capital dried up quickly during the 2020 global pandemic and investors appetites have only now begun to return to pre-pandemic levels.

Yet, the trends are clear over the first four Project Sage reports—gender lens investing is a growing consideration among providers of early stage capital. According to the GLI research, gender lens investing can be categorized in several ways. Gender lens investors may focus on advancing more women in finance and leadership, including increasing the number of female fund managers and limited partners or increasing the number of women on corporate boards. Investments may also concentrate on products and services which specifically impact women's lives. And still others look at investing in companies actively improving employment for women or increasing the diversity of a company's supply chain. Some funds include a "gender lens mandate" directly in their fund thesis while others imbed GLI as a "consideration" in their investment strategy. Regardless, there is clear evidence that GLI is a global movement increasing the amount of capital managed by and investing in women.

Why is Gender Lens Investing as a category important? The growth of women-led firms and more capital being invested through a gender lens is beginning to change the landscape of early stage investing. GLI investors are more likely to adjust their language and approach in pitches and meetings with female founders to be less gender biased and more supportive. They may see undiscovered opportunities in underserved markets, particularly those for which they have a personal affinity or experience. Some women VCs have added specific clauses to investment term sheets such as requiring companies to establish DEI (diversity, equity, inclusion) policies or impact agreements. And still others actively help their portfolio companies consider how to establish and expand inclusive management practices or increase the diversification of their leadership teams.

Proponents of GLI outline several key market advantages offered by investing with a gender lens. First, if the fund or entity is led by women, you gain a unique perspective which is not held by a majority of investors. As those who make most consumer decisions in households as well as have experienced healthcare, technology, or other industry gaps in addressing issues and concerns specific to women, a gender lens offers a window into overlooked market opportunities. Women-led ventures are now addressing taboo topics such as "period poverty" to expand equal access to feminine hygiene products (Aunt Flow), women's sexual health (Joylux), or menopause (Gennev).

Second, women investors and entrepreneurs are drawn to creating and investing in products and services with double or even triple bottom lines—encompassing economic, social, and environmental impact. The majority of JumpFund's investments have broad reaching social or environmental impact, even though that is not necessarily part of our investment thesis. Our portfolio includes Funding U, a company dedicated to increasing access to "last gap" student loans and Stony Creek Colors, which produces natural indigo dye for the denim industry, to make fashion more sustainable. Other JumpFund companies are leveraging technology to do good including Resilia, a SAAS (software as a service) platform which helps nonprofits build their capacity and funders assess their impact. And Worthy, which offers affordable, $10 bonds to those who have not previously had access to passive wealth building and re-invests those dollars into loans for other "main street" enterprises.

Sadly, we lost Suzanne Biegel, the godmother of GLI in the spring of 2023. Yet, her important research continues through a consortium of universities (UPenn, Harvard, Columbia) and through a new fund, Heading for Change, to further advance gender equality and climate solutions. Her legacy lives on in the movement she helped create and her groundbreaking research and advocacy will influence many more to consider the importance of investing with a gender lens.

Women Investing in Women

Venture fund and angel investor groups come in all shapes, sizes, and follow a wide variety of investment theses. There are funds focused solely on a single industry such as EdTech, consumer goods, or life sciences. Many early stage investors direct funding only in their cities or regions for purposes of local economic development. Our brother fund, the Chattanooga Renaissance Fund, had a specific goal to invest in startups growing in our own city. The JumpFund saw an opportunity to invest through a "gender lens" and to intentionally seek out high potential companies run by strong women. And we purposely decided to be regionally focused in our investments as we witnessed a huge gap in funding for women particularly in the Southeast. At the time we founded our first fund, there were no other female-focused investment firms in this region of the U.S. so we knew we could have greater impact with our relatively smaller dollars by narrowing our geographic aperture.

I can't tell you how many cocktail party conversations I've had since starting JumpFund, generally talking with a man, which go something like this:

Man: "What is your fund's investment thesis?"

Me: "Well, we are a women-led firm which invests in women-led ventures."

Man: "Isn't investing in only women narrowing your scope of opportunity? Shouldn't you be looking for the best deals regardless of gender?"

Me: "Well, shouldn't you? How many women led companies do you have in your portfolio? We see this as an arbitrage opportunity since women do not have access to capital at anywhere near the same levels as men and data shows that women-led ventures outperform their male counterparts. In fact, women receive less than 3% of all venture capital yet produce 63% higher returns on investment."

Generally, this is a conversation stopper, unless, of course, they want to "mansplain" further. Alternatively, they offer up a woman-led company they would love to introduce me to, but haven't invested in themselves. Not exactly a ringing endorsement!

Early on in our fund's development, conversations about our intention to invest in women-only often turned to perceived deficits as to why female founders may not be receiving equitable capital to grow their companies. While 40% of new companies in the U.S. are started by women every year the number of those bringing in over $1mm in annual revenue represent a much lower percentage. Some of this has to do with women predominantly starting smaller scale, "lifestyle" businesses, that may support one's family and a few employees but may not scale to produce outsized returns for potential investors. It is the women starting businesses with the potential to scale into millions in revenue who do not have access to adequate funding sources to seed and grow their startup ventures.

Women are often seen as "risk averse" and lacking in the "confidence" to successfully build a high growth venture. Women are also viewed as not having the adequate skill sets to lead a company—business acumen, financial knowledge, engineering capabilities, an innovative mindset. Contrary to these myths, women hold the majority of advanced degrees in the U.S. especially in sciences and other fields relative to innovation and entrepreneurship. According to the American Enterprise Institute, women earned a majority of doctoral degrees in 2019 for the 11th straight year and outnumber men in graduate school 141 to 100.[6] And, while some women may not have the blustering egos and over-confidence found in their male counterparts, they do have innovative ideas and plans to execute on them if given the opportunity.

Early stage investors are generally betting on the jockey, not the horse. If we don't have confidence out of the gate that a founder has "what it takes" to build a successful company and take it to the finish line, bringing in strong capital returns for investors, then we are unlikely to place our bet. Ideas are a dime a dozen, successful leaders are not.

Yet, personal biases often come into play when investors are judging the potential future success of a founder. When we were starting our first fund and gathering data on why it was important to focus on investing in women, we came across a now widely publicized Harvard study on gender bias in venture capital.[7] The study had highly prepared, Harvard Business School-educated founders, pitching their companies to groups of investors. Time and again, the white males would garner the investments over the female contenders. Feedback such as "I saw myself in him" or "he made me feel confident in our investment" resounded from the investors while the women received questions about their ability to lead the company, their readiness to "do what it takes," and their general capabilities around finance, business development, and sales.

The JumpFund wanted to offer something different. We wanted to plant a flag firmly in the ground that we were biased in the opposite way, primarily to break down the stereotypes that there were not investable female founders and company CEOs out there. We literally had other male-led firms tell us time and again that they *would* invest in women if only they could "find" them. Or, more accurately, if female founders showed up at their doors they wouldn't turn them away. Unfortunately, these firms' portfolios will continue to be full of majority male-led companies if they do not proactively consider their own biases and intentionally seek out more diversity on founding teams.

Another investor bias study from Dana Kanze and researchers at Columbia University emerged as we began investing out of our first fund and considered the types of questions asked of founders by investors during pitch competitions. These questions fell decidedly into two categories depending on the gender of the founder. Men were asked more "promotional" questions, such as how they planned to acquire customers, what is their strategy to monetize their product, or what major milestones are they planning to hit in the next year. Women were asked more "preventative" questions such as how many active users they had, how long would it take to break even, or how predictable are their future cash flows.[8]

All are reasonable questions to ask a company while in diligence, but not generally during a ten-minute pitch competition. The preventative questions were designed to call out gaps in expertise, weakness in the company strategy, or reaffirm biases about areas in which an investor may perceive a woman to be less versed. The promotion questions helped to reinforce investor perceptions of their hopes, ideals and achievements of the male entrepreneurs. In the end, while the companies in the competition were all pre-screened for similar quality, stage, and potential, the male presenters garnered **five times** more capital for their ventures than the women on stage. This study is one of many which highlights how gender plays a significant part in potential funding for early stage companies.

VCs Frame Questions in Two Different Ways

Promotion questions focus on potential gains, whereas prevention questions focus on potential losses. VCs tend to ask the former of men and the latter of women.

TOPIC	PROMOTION	PREVENTION
Customers	Acquisition Example question: "How do you want to acquire customers?"	Retention Example question: "How many daily and monthly active users do you have?"
Income statement	Sales "How do you plan to monetize this?"	Margins "How long will it take you to break even?"
Market	Size "Do you think that your target market is a growing one?"	Share "Is it a defensible business wherein other people can't come into the space to take share?"
Projections	Growth "What major milestones are you targeting for this year?"	Stability "How predictable are your future cash flows?"
Strategy	Vision "What's the brand vision?"	Execution "Are you planning to Turing test this?"
Management	Entrepreneur "Can you tell us a bit about yourself?"	Team "How much of this are you actually doing in-house?"

SOURCE DANA KANZE, LAURA HUANG, MARK A. CONLEY, AND E. TORY HIGGINS   © HBR.ORG

Mad, Bad and Dangerous

When I'm interviewed about JumpFund's story or questioned about why we invest in women, I prefer to focus on the advantages female founders have over their male counterparts, not the perceived deficits. In 2015, a few years into the investment period of our first fund, First Round Capital, a founder-focused, seed stage investment fund with early investment in Uber and Square, released a ten-year study of their portfolio's performance. The first finding in a deep dive of data about their companies' success was that female founders consistently outperformed their male counterparts—by 63%! This was based on their analysis of the return on their investment in all-male teams versus those with at least one female founder.[9]

First Round's research revealed clear links between how women build and run companies versus men. In part due to the dearth of capital available for women-led companies, women tend to be more capital efficient, making the money they have to grow their companies last longer. For similar reasons, female founded companies are also often at a slightly later stage when they secure their first outside investment capital, having "bootstrapped" their company to that point. And women tend to be better company managers which can be a difficult transition for a founder—moving from the "idea" person to building out and managing a team to successfully run a company. Women understand the importance of having a wide variety of thought and experience on their teams and their company cultures tend to be more supportive of diverse team members who impact the design, development and ultimately sales of products and services, broadening their potential client base.

> We've been fortunate to back many companies with female founders and women-founded companies represent a greater percentage of our investments than the national VC average. Our investments in companies with at least one female founder were meaningfully outperforming our investments in all-male teams. **Companies with a female founder performed 63% better than our investments**

with all-male founding teams. *And, if you look at First Round's top 10 investments of all time based on value created for investors, three of those teams have at least one female founder—far outpacing the percentage of female tech founders in general.*

—First Round Capital Report, 2015

Another part of the narrative around women entrepreneurs we sought to change was that women and girls are not interested in running businesses. According to the Women's Business Enterprise National Council, there are 13 million women-owned businesses in the U.S., representing almost half of all businesses started annually. And the number of women-owned firms has grown by 114% in the last two decades, as reported by Inc. magazine.

The JumpFund wanted to find ways in our own community to tell this story, by promoting and celebrating women and girls as entrepreneurs. We had met a young startup genius, Stacey Ferrara who came to Chattanooga to speak as part of a Thiel Fellows program, that our partner Tiffanie had been instrumental in bringing to town through her work with Sandbox, a global next gen startup leadership network. Stacey was a 21 year old who had started her first tech company straight out of high school with her brother and garnered her first $1M in investment from Sir Richard Branson. This whip-smart entrepreneur was featured in a 2016 documentary film, *She Started It,* which was written and directed by Nora Poggi, a French journalist and filmmaker. After meeting Stacey and learning about her role in the film we saw a chance to highlight other young female founders and reached out to Nora to discuss including Chattanooga on the film's multi-city U.S. tour.

At the same time, JumpFund began to work with a local girl's school on a program their new, innovative headmaster had developed in collaboration with the Company Lab, called Mad, Bad, and Dangerous (aka MBD). This summer program was designed to attract girls from across the city to "ditch expectations and start something" and to think bigger and bolder about innovative solutions for business as well as becoming their own entrepreneurs. Leading with catchy, emboldening phrases such a "we're the new American muscle," and "the fairer gender never surrenders" as well as a #girlpreneurs social media campaign, MBD's mission was to help women and girls "understand the power of entrepreneurship and believe in their ideas while learning to put them into action."

The JumpFund partners participated as advisors, mentors, speakers, and even hosted a booth at the MBD summit for the girls to "crowdfund" their businesses, with the winners taking home the pot of money collectively contributed by their supporters (all those proud moms, dads, cousins, and aunts). Shelley gave her "Lead Like a Girl" TEDx talk and Cory and Stefanie served as judges for the pitch competitions. In conjunction with MBD, JumpFund hosted a public event for the U.S. tour of the documentary film She Started It, with guest speakers Nora Poggi and another entrepreneur featured in the film, Sheena Allen, CEO of CapWay in Atlanta. Sheena also volunteered to speak with and mentor some of the girls at the school during her visit. These types of collaborations helped us to elevate the conversation around whether girls and women were really even interested in starting and growing businesses. In fact, they were hungry and eager to jump at the chance to showcase their entrepreneurial chops!

Southeast Female Founder Spotlight:
Sara Blakely & SPANX

When asked early on if we could name any successful female-led startups in the Southeast, SPANX always rose to the top of our list. Sara Blakely, the Atlanta-based founder of internationally known "shapewear" brand Spanx, is a prime example of a woman who had to hustle and bootstrap her idea and company, growing it into a billion dollar brand. Investors just didn't get her new fangled girdle, which was essentially the control-top portion of traditional panty hose. Pitching the product to major retailers, Sara would go into the dressing room and literally present a "before and after" version of herself wearing Spanx, finally persuading Neiman Marcus to be the first store to carry the product. Now Spanx is a household name and has a full line of undergarments, swimsuits, and even jeans which you can find in stand-alone Spanx retail stores as well as Target and most nationwide retailers.

Sara's hustle and marketing savvy with her background in sales, helped propel Spanx to rapidly become an international name brand. In 2000, after sending some of the Spanx products to Oprah Winfrey, the product was named one of her "favorite things" and a year later Blakely picked up a lucrative sales deal with QVC. In its first year of sales, the company generated $4 million in revenue rapidly scaling to $10 million its second year. In 2012, Blakely made the cover of Forbes as the youngest self-made female billionaire. She maintains that beyond the $5,000 in savings she initially spent to get Spanx off the ground, she has never taken outside investment. In 2006 she launched the Spanx by Sara Blakely Foundation to support women in entrepreneurship, education, and the arts and joined the "Giving Pledge" along with other billionaires to give away half their wealth. The Spanx Foundation has supported numerous business incubators and demo days, especially in and around Atlanta, including one co-hosted with the Fearless Fund, one of JumpFund's gender lens investor partners.

In 2021, Sara Blakely inked a significant private equity deal with Blackstone becoming majority shareholder and valuing the company at $1.2 billion. After the deal was signed, Blakely posted on social media *"People have asked me for 20 years, when will you sell Spanx? And for 20 years I would say, 'I'll just know.' Well that day is today. I will remain a significant shareholder and continue to help the business fulfill its potential, as well as continue to fulfill my greatest passion—elevating women."*

The Gap Table

A cap (capitalization) table is a running tally of all investors in a company with their percentage ownership and cost basis. The "Gap Table" has been a term used to indicate the absence of women or women-led firms as investors in venture-backed companies. The JumpFund is one of many emerging female-led firms working to change this phenomenon. According to Jessica Peltz-Zatulove, co-founder of Women in VC, "when you change the composition of the fund managers controlling the capital, it expands the likelihood of underrepresented founders getting funded—and as a byproduct, the types of products, goods, or opportunities that get brought to market."

The dearth of women in finance has been a long term issue in our capitalist economy. Women are few and far between even now on Wall Street or leading banking or financial firms, and certainly absent when it comes to the very male-centric, ego-filled world of venture capital.[10] In 2020, the percentage of venture capital partners in the U.S. who are women was a mere 4.9%.[11] And only half of those were *founding* partners of venture capital firms, according to Kelly Reeser with Tech Farms Capital. But as more women enter this field, there is a growing network of industry professionals who are committed to collaboration, deal sharing, and promoting diversity on company cap tables and boards of directors.

In the Southeast, the number of women in venture capital and as angel investors is growing but not nearly where it needs to be. A 2019 report by #BuildintheSE, a group of women tracking the rise of Southeast firms attracting venture capital as well as the dearth of women in venture, found that in Tennessee there were a total of 18 women in venture firms of which only 12 were at the partner level and JumpFund general partners represented seven of those.[12] When we launched our first fund, we had very few female role models in this industry. While we were not seeing women in regional accelerator programs or on demo stages, we were certainly not seeing any women investing in early stage ventures across the Southeast. While we knew that women had the capital and certainly had the financial savvy to apply to this work, there seemed to be major roadblocks to engaging them as investors or leaning in further to lead venture capital firms.

Even with more women joining the ranks of venture capital firms and others starting their own, the VC world remains a boys club. A well-known Harvard study looked at the implicit bias exhibited in male investors when pitched by men or women. It found that "investors preferred pitches presented by male entrepreneurs compared to pitches made by female entrepreneurs, even when the content of the pitch was the exact same."[13] Even worse, horror stories have surfaced from female founders who were felt up, propositioned, or sexually harassed when pitching their companies to male VCs.[14]

At demo days where entrepreneurs take the stage and pitch their companies, several of our JumpFund founders have related how they were propositioned instead of being taken seriously about their business ideas. Instead of digging into a female founder's product development, team structure, or customer retention, a potential investor might offer to buy her a drink, brush his hands on her back or hip, or comment on her pretty eyes. In one instance, when one of JumpFund's very own partners was pitching her startup on stage at a large entrepreneurial conference in Nashville, a judge from Texas, who had already downed a few beers, led with a question: "Where did you buy that pretty blue dress? I want to get one for my wife," instead of asking about her business pitch. Shelley went on to win the competition and a $50,000 investment in her company, but the comment from the judge was repeated far and wide during the rest of the conference. For some it seemed like a good-natured joke, but to many of us it encapsulated exactly what our female entrepreneurs faced on a daily basis—dismissal, devaluing, and disrespect.

The "Me Too" movement in 2018-2019 also shed a bright light on male sexism and predatory behavior in the workplace, particularly in the male-power sectors of the entertainment industry and big tech. In 2015, Gimlet Media's new StartUp podcast featured a series following the 20-something female founders of the Dating Ring, a new matchmaking app, and their challenges as outsiders in the male-dominated world of Silicon Valley. Their vivid accounts of the bias, sexism and outright lecherous behavior these young women experienced on their road to raise capital are similar to so many other accounts we have heard and unfortunately continue to hear from women fundraising for their companies and building their businesses—whether the interactions be with investors or clients.

Finding Our Tribe

When the founders of The JumpFund began to explore this unfamiliar and often hostile world of venture capital as we were building our own fund, we knew we needed allies and mentors who could offer a different perspective. We wanted to be a "dolphin tank" versus a shark tank, and serve as an open door and sounding board for female founders. We wanted to challenge the status quo nature of predatory venture capital and create a nurturing environment for founders and investors to ask questions they might feel uncomfortable posing in a room dominated by men. And, we wanted to position ourselves as a transparent early stage investment firm which valued shared learning and building successful ventures with a new kind of corporate culture.

Our first mentors and role models were found in Golden Seeds, one of the original networks of women investing in women. Since 2004, Golden Seeds has been one of the most active early stage investor groups focusing solely on female founders with more than $175M invested in over 240 companies and a membership of 300+ mostly female investors spanning the U.S. When we reached out to them as a nascent fund, they welcomed us with open arms. We spent our first year learning from Golden Seeds through their robust angel investor training program in New York and attending their annual venture summits where they gathered their members and founders for several days of company updates and dinners at Golden Seeds' partners homes throughout Manhattan.

Sitting across the room from the former CMO of *Ms. Magazine* at our first "Introduction to Angel Investing" seminar was a heady experience. We had found our tribe—here were "women like us" interested in solely investing in other women. They were bankers, lawyers, former CEOs and marketing executives. They had capital to deploy and were definitely interested in the financial return opportunity of investing in high growth startups. But they also cared about the lack of access to capital for women-led companies and how their investments could move the needle on these statistics. This was not another charity, this was business, and these women wanted to challenge the boys club of venture capital.

For the first several years, JumpFund joined Golden Seeds as a corporate affiliate to increase our deal flow as well as share Southeast ventures in our pipeline with their investor group. At our inaugural gathering of our fund's investors, we invited Loretta McCarthy, a Golden Seeds founding partner to speak to the group on the imperative and opportunity of investing in women. She gave a powerful pitch about "why women" and the success Golden Seeds had experienced in finding and investing solely in female founders.

As women, we quickly understood the importance of educating ourselves in this new field in order to feel more confident in establishing our first fund. Through Golden Seeds we also learned about the Angel Capital Association (ACA), a national network of funds, angel investor groups and individuals offering educational resources and colleagueship in this industry. Betsy Brown and I attended our first ACA summit in 2014 along with a band of women from Golden Seeds, where we were definitely among the minority. I love to recount that at that first summit we attended, there was actually a line for the men's room and not the women's (unheard of at a conference of over 900!). Yet it was at ACA that we discovered the growing number of women launching their own funds and networks across the country, further expanding our tribe.

Growing Women's Capital

Over the next several years, we were part of a movement at the Angel Capital Association (ACA) that saw a growth in women's leadership in angel funds and networks as well as within the leadership of the ACA organization itself.

We began meeting and hosting panels discussing the importance of investing in diverse teams and engaging more women as angel investors. We met other women like us who were interested in both the returns and impact their capital could have. Together we formalized a new network at the ACA called Growing Women's Capital, which began to host its own annual gatherings as well as a monthly virtual call to syndicate deals in which we were invested. In 2019, the annual ACA summit focused on equity and impact at the behest of the growing number of angel investors with impact lens investment theses. At that event, one of the keynote speakers was a Dana Kanze, a researcher from Columbia University who delivered a scathing presentation on the difference in "promotion vs. prevention" questions asked by investors of male vs. female founders. We knew at that point that the issue of access to capital for women, while by no means solved, was profoundly being recognized and women were beginning to take hold of the narrative as angel investors themselves.

Beside cutting through the rampant sexism and gender bias often found in all-male investor groups, why is it important for more women to be in venture capital? And with all of its evident baggage, why would we embrace this term over the more palatable "angel investor" moniker? The JumpFund founders felt that while we were technically a venture capital firm, deploying the investments of our limited partners, we gravitated to the angel investor sandbox which was a more welcoming, supportive environment, and although still biased, at least willing to readily change. In the past ten years, the number of women identifying as angel investors has risen from 5% when JumpFund launched in 2013 to almost 30% in less than ten years. This is in part due to the growing number of angel funds and networks built by women for women. These women-led angel groups acknowledge the need to increase access for first-time female investors with lower investment minimums, create supportive learning communities, and offer education and training.

Women make at least 80% of all consumer decisions in the market, including electronics and automobiles.[15] If that is the case, then having women as partners in venture firms or leading angel groups that assess the market potential and viability of nascent companies is critical to understanding a product or service's opportunity. We have had male investors relate that when pitched about a woman-centric product or service they either shy away or ask their wives, and ultimately do not invest. Women investors are often wrongly portrayed as being mostly interested in consumer product companies, especially in the beauty sector or in women's healthcare, or those offering services predominantly for female customers. The JumpFund is proud that our very first investment was in a sports fan engagement company—not typically considered women's area of expertise or interest.

Instead, it is more likely that women investors are interested in investing in companies with a higher purpose, such as social or environmental impact. They look for "double bottom line" companies that consider not only how to make strong returns, but those which have the potential to benefit or change the world. Next Wave Impact, another gender lens fund in which I served on the investment committee, was founded in 2017 on the principle that more women might be attracted to early stage investing if the investment thesis of the fund was focused through an impact lens. With over 100 female investors, Next Wave has invested in more than 15 "impact" ventures ranging from community solar technology to STEM education platforms. Not surprisingly, all of these companies have either a female CEO or co-founder, not necessarily a criteria for Next Wave, but as a group of women investors gender diverse leadership remains an important factor.

This leads to another reason more women are needed in early stage investing: women invest in women. The Jump-Fund's early premise was that if men were not investing in women, then women should start doing it for themselves. A 2018 Kauffman report shows that female VC partners invested in twice as many more female founding teams at the early stages, with the results being more pronounced in Computer Science (63%) and Consumer-facing start-ups (108%). The study looked at nearly 57,000 venture capital partner investments across thousands of firms where 80% of venture investment decisions are made by men. Furthermore, the $147 billion raised by all-male founders exceeded the amount of venture capital put into women-led teams for the previous 19 years combined.[16]

There is also an enormous market opportunity being missed by companies who do not understand nor invest in the needs and demands of female consumers. Women continue to feel underserved in the marketplace, from healthcare to convenience products that would help them be more successful, healthy, and productive. This problem is not new—a 2008 Boston Consulting Group study looked at the unmet needs of women who then controlled over $20 trillion in global consumer spending. From SUVs that are more utility-focused (think carpooling and grocery runs) to fitness options that fit into packed daily routines, women should be driving the development of products and services that meet their needs. In the oft-cited 2009 article, "The Female Economy" by Michael Silverstein and Kate Sayre, they found that "globally, women control $20 trillion in annual consumer spending, and that figure could climb as high as $28 trillion in the next five years. In aggregate, women represent a growth market bigger than China and India combined—more than twice as big, in fact." Given those numbers, according to the report, it would be foolish to ignore or underestimate the female consumer. [17]

Women-led angel funds have been quietly growing companies with female-focused products and services and have helped launch a whole new category called Fem-Tech. Gennev, a woman-led startup focusing exclusively on the need for products and support networks for women going through menopause, has been predominantly invested in by female funds and networks, such as Portfolia's aptly named FemTech Fund. FemTech companies such as Rosy and Joylux, both addressing women's sexual health, are making waves and gaining traction with gender lens funds, and traditional venture capital is beginning to take notice.

The recent Global Pandemic brought to light huge social and economic disparities, especially for women who had to juggle home-schooling and at-home childcare with work. Some 80% of all jobs lost in 2020 were attributed to women, and women of color were hit the hardest. With no childcare, schooling moving online at home for months on end, and often the double duty of caring for aging parents, women could not also shoulder full-time jobs. Often women did not have the luxury of remote work, especially as many hold lower paid, menial positions in our workforce, and lost their jobs entirely. According to Emily Martin, VP for education and workplace justice at the National Women's Law Center: "The pandemic's impact on women and women of color, in particular, threatens women's economic security in the future. This country is really facing fundamental questions—whether we're going to make long-term investments in child care, paid leave, and paid sick days that help ensure that caregiving responsibilities don't have this terrible economic impact."[18]

The JumpFund was proud that all of our female founders were able to keep their companies above water during the pandemic, but we know the struggles these women faced as we experienced them ourselves. Data shows that women entrepreneurs were also harder hit than men during the pandemic, with the added struggle of raising capital during a time of deep uncertainty and continued gender bias. According to the *Harvard Business Review,* "some speculate that the pandemic made investors more wary of risks and more likely to stick to their existing networks—which is very much a "boys club" and tougher for women to break into. And even when going outside their networks, many investors may be sticking with "pattern-matching habits," seeking the same kinds of companies that they've supported in the past, which are often tech companies led by men."[19]

Given this ongoing divide, it is important to consider how we are mentoring and supporting the next generation of women in venture capital. With my background in education, especially mentoring young women at the business school, I knew there was a terrific pipeline of young women in finance, entrepreneurship, and even human resources potentially looking for interesting internships. Over the years, JumpFund has employed several amazing interns and even cultivated a few who have gone on to pursue a future in VC or entrepreneurship. Our first intern, Eller Mallchok Kelliher, was a biology major at Dickinson College, where she served on the school's student venture fund. This experience, combined with her internship at JumpFund, gave her a taste of the world of startup investing and she took a leap into this work full-time at JumpStart Foundry (no relation to JumpFund) a health tech venture incubator in Nashville. She now serves as Investor in Residence at LaunchTN, our statewide entrepreneurial ecosystem engine.

In 2018, we hired Kenzie Butera Davis as a fund associate where she handled our investor communications, social media, pipeline and due diligence management, and other back office support. Kenzie was in the process of completing her dual degree in Women's Studies and Entrepreneurship at UT Chattanooga, and had just finished a fellowship at the Company Lab, our local business accelerator. During her time with JumpFund, she participated in a next-gen program with Venture University, deep-diving on all aspects of venture capital. After two years with us, Kenzie took the leap and launched her own venture, Maro—a parenting app for addressing the "tough issues of growing up" with your kids—which was named one of 46 top startups to watch in 2021 by VCs according to *Business Insider* and recently won the top prize out of 900 global companies at ASU/GSV, the largest edtech conference in the world. We are proud of these two young women making great strides as the next generation of women in venture capital and entrepreneurship.

As more female managed funds and angel investor networks come to the forefront, the landscape is changing for women-led ventures. Unfortunately, in the past eight years as women are growing their ranks in this industry, the percentage of venture capital going to women has stayed stagnant. It will take more women moving up into later stage venture firms, funding companies with millions of dollars versus thousands, to really begin to see the impact of more capital going to teams with at least one female founder.

Diversifying Your Portfolio

In the investment world, portfolio diversification is often a goal of financial advisors to ensure clients' assets are spread across a wide variety of investments to mitigate market and personal economic risk. This same strategy can be applied to early stage investing, looking at investments across industries (life sciences, education technology, clean tech, etc) or stage of companies (seed stage to Series C and beyond). But what about diversification based on company leadership? Investing with an eye towards the balance of gender, race, and other marginalized groups to create a portfolio that reflects the true depth and breadth of the entire marketplace, not just one narrow, privileged view.

Savvy angel investors understand that there are unique advantages to investing in underrepresented and heretofore underfunded founders. A diverse founding team offers a wider perspective on the market, which, as we've mentioned before, is actually dominated by female consumers. Certain sectors of the population, including women, people of color, and LGBTQIA+ people are often left out of decision-making and product development at the earliest stages when it is most important. Some founders are now capitalizing on these blue ocean market opportunities such as in women's health and wellness or non-binary fashion. But what if more companies were developing their products and services with ALL members of our diverse world in mind? How big would the "total addressable market" be then?

When starting JumpFund and planting our flag firmly to serve women entrepreneurs, we were met with suggestions that we were limiting our market potential. And, more importantly, the male-led firms we spoke with felt they were decidedly gender agnostic and would embrace diversity if it came calling. Yet, to change the game, we knew we needed to have a more intentional and direct approach. In order to reverse years, even generations of bias, you have to seek out diversity, not let it just come to you. Women and other historically underrepresented groups that had not seen the same access to capital did not feel welcomed or invited to even apply to the existing male-dominated world of venture capital. The door may have been left open a crack to "allow" for diversity, but few marginalized founders were brave enough to knock.

Instead, JumpFund and other groups like ours, have opened the door wide to all those not originally invited to the party. By announcing that we had dollars specifically to invest in women-led ventures, a wider aperture of founders naturally flowed. Our first investment had a founding team with a white female CMO, a white male CTO, and a black male CEO. Our first positive exit, Partpic, was led by a black woman, with a black female CTO, and a broadly diverse team spanning gender and race. Other groups such as Next Wave Impact Fund, in collaboration with over 300 like-minded investment partners, launched a Founders of Color Showcase at the Angel Capital Association's annual summit, which thus far has featured more than 35 diverse founding teams.

There are also a growing number of new venture capital firms specifically focused on founders of color, particularly out of Atlanta, the U.S. capital of black business and wealth generation. Fearless Fund, started by Arian Simone, Keisha Knight Pulliam (who played Rudy Huxtable on the Cosby Show), and Ayana Parsons, has grown to over $25mm in assets and is backed by PayPal, JP Morgan Chase, and MasterCard. Since 2019, Fearless has invested more than $27M in over 40 ventures run by women of color, and JumpFund is proud to be one of their original investors. Collab Capital, co-founded by Jewel Burks Solomon and partners Barry Givens and Justin Dawkins raised a $50M fund dedicated to "transforming genius into generational wealth" and targeting black tech founders. Jewel is also the head of Google for Startups and was the founder/CEO of Partpic, in which JumpFund invested, which was sold to Amazon in 2016. These women are paving the way for a new generation of diverse fund managers and redirecting capital to founders of color.

It is difficult to break out of your comfort zone and be

more intentional about the personal and professional circles you build. Early stage investing is a relational game, with founders and investors meeting up at conferences, events, bars, or golf courses. If you are an investor truly interested in seeking out companies with female or BIPOC team leadership or helping your current portfolio companies address a wider market, consider how you might purposely engage with a wider diversity of founders. Attend events and accelerator programs supporting diverse entrepreneurs such as Morgan Stanley's Multicultural Accelerator, the Founders of Color Showcase, or the Zane Access program. Seek out local economic development groups in your region that are supporting and investing in diverse startup teams. Lean on gender lens or BIPOC-focused investment firms such as Golden Seeds, Portfolia, or the Black Angel Tech Fund for deal flow and due diligence on prospective companies. Or, consider launching a version of Village Capital's VC Pathways designed to move "beyond friends and family round" and increase the "social capital" of Black, Latinx, and female founders to provide greater access to early stage funding from angel and institutional investors.[20] In 2018 Village Capital hosted a series of purpose-driven events in cities across the U.S. to provide opportunities for diverse founders to meet socially with interested investors and cultivate deeper connections.

Diversity does build on diversity. And more importantly, diversity leads to stronger return potential for investors. A 2017 American Angel Report by the Wharton School found that racially diverse teams outperform on ROI (return on investment) by as much as an additional 1x, much like earlier findings about gender balance on founding teams. Next Wave Impact Fund I realized its first positive returns with a company led by a black male founder, ConnXus, focused on supply chain diversity and compliance.[21]

There is money to be made in under-capitalized markets, especially where companies are excelling despite the odds. Diverse founding teams produce a more open and accepting corporate culture which can often lead to fewer lawsuits and happier employees down the line. These companies in turn offer new market perspectives that have not previously been considered including Black women's hair and beauty products (Carol's Daughter or Mielle Organics), safe dating networks for the LGBTQ community (Grindr and HER), or tools to assist at-home caregivers with their aging parents (Unaliwear). What you find may surprise and delight you, but more importantly, offer an ROI that other investors are yet to discover.

Unfortunately, as of this book's publishing, several lawsuits are making their way through the courts challenging groups, funds, and even corporations expressly investing in diversity. The Fearless Fund's grants to support women of color (underwritten by MasterCard) and Hello Alice's small business grants for black business owners (underwritten by Progressive Insurance) are among several programs facing legal action brought by the same group that won the Supreme Court case banning affirmative action. The battle for equal access to capital is real and ongoing and needs more of us who value diversity and inclusion to step up and move our dollars in support.

Women and Money

When we launched our first fund, it was clear that many of the women we were recruiting to invest had never had any real control over decision-making with their assets, whether they were owned jointly or not. We would hear that their husband thought our venture too risky—investing in first-time fund managers and specifically in women, was too niche, too unproven, very much out of their wheelhouse. Yet, these same men would invest directly in their friend's startup ventures or with groups of other men in funds or networks investing in early stage companies. They would let their wives control their family's philanthropic giving, but not anything that might carry a return on investment potential.

Several women we spoke with also turned the decision on whether or not to invest in JumpFund over to their financial advisors. As many of us in early stage investing know, most traditional advisors do not like the risks inherent in private equity, especially with smaller, unproven funds. They are more comfortable with advising their clients on which securities, mutual funds, or bonds to invest in and often make a commission on the purchase of these assets. There is nothing in it for these advisors to suggest their clients consider investing a small portion of their portfolio directly in ventures that excite them or bring them joy. There are few financial cheerleaders for women who are interested in specifically investing in other women and see the advantages of doing so.

As a group of women who had control of our own assets or had supportive spouses who understood both the risks and potential rewards of our investment thesis, it was hard for us to watch other women walk away from what we felt was a bold, unprecedented opportunity to put their money where their heart was. If they were giving to charities and nonprofits that supported the social and economic advancement of women and girls, why would they NOT invest directly in women-led businesses, paying it forward even further and potentially earning a return which they could then redirect to more charitable giving? It seemed at cross purposes to us, but many women did not feel empowered to make money decisions around investments as they did with philanthropy, sometimes giving millions of dollars to causes they cared about while a $30,000 minimum commitment to our first fund seemed out of the question.

The majority of our investors turned out to be those women who had control over their own assets, women who had been in business or had accumulated wealth moving up the corporate ladder. They saw the "arbitrage" opportunity we were presenting as they knew how under-resourced women in business were and that they could be just as successful or more so than male entrepreneurs. They also understood and many had even experienced the huge disadvantages, bias, and sexism in business and particularly venture capital for women and they wanted to be on the front lines of changing the game and creating a new corporate culture with women at the helm.

Why are so many women uncomfortable with money? Why do we have a love/hate relationship with it? And why, if more than 50% of all wealth will transfer to women in the next ten years, do we still rely on others to tell us what to do with it?

I met Janine Firpo, author of *Activate Your Money* (2021) when I joined her and nine other women as leaders of the Investment Committee (similar to a general partner) of Next Wave Impact Fund in 2017. Next Wave Impact, as I detail later in this book, was a fund model designed to draw more women into angel investing with an emphasis on education and learning by doing along with a like-minded group of women. Janine, who came from a successful corporate and nonprofit career, most recently with the Gates Foundation, decided to write her new book about her own journey with money as well as stories and anecdotes from other women who wanted to do "more" with their money.

As she found in her research, women have a complicated relationship with money and generally feel a lack of control or independence about their finances. This could be because of a division of labor within the household and the majority of money decisions being made by the spouse, father, or other men in the family. Or, they turn their assets over to an advisor with whom they feel equal unease asking questions or providing direction as to how they would like to invest.

And, it is not only women investors that have a tricky and often negative relationship with money. Female entrepreneurs, who are praised for their lean company strategy and self-funding longer before seeking venture capital, are also victims of the "gender equity gap." Once women do seek funding, they are more likely to give up more of their company more quickly than their male counterparts or agree to more egregious terms that dilute their ownership over time and end up with very little of their own company returns in the end.

According to Melissa Widen at First Women's Bank in Chicago, women tend to retain only 40 cents to every dollar of their companies than male-led companies. Instead of exploring alternative financing strategies, such as debt or revenue-based financing, which help retain founder ownership, women are caught in a web of raising capital that they have limited access to in the first place and thus less favorable terms and investment partners. There are also instances of predatory angels and VCs that take advantage of women's discomfort with the financial side of their business and end up taking over the business and displacing the woman at the helm or threatening lawsuits that could bring down their company.

Female entrepreneurs also often have difficulty "owning" the financial side of their business or speaking clearly to their financial, pro forma modeling when pitching their companies. I have coached many founders on this subject and encouraged them to find help putting together strong predictive cash flow and growth models but more importantly, really understand the levers in their business that will generate strong returns. Angel investors are interested in rapid, "hockey stick" growth and you need to make a strong case from the outset on how your product or service will achieve certain metrics. The JumpFund's growth trajectory standard was "tell us how you will grow to a minimum $20M company in five years or less." Other investors might put a much more aggressive marker, such as $100M, or tie metrics to market comparisons. Building a business that attracts investors is all about setting big, hairy audacious goals and mapping out how you will achieve them and make a return within a fairly short window of time. Women entrepreneurs need to own their metrics as well as have a clear handle on business finance to be successful.

The JumpFund and other female angel investors are working to change the dynamic of women and money, one investor and entrepreneur at a time. We help our entrepreneurs think through their capitalization strategy at an early stage and run scenarios that help mitigate future risk of heavy dilution. We have coached many companies who have come to us for investment on how to create stronger pro formas (financial projections) that match investor appetites while also clearly articulating how they will scale their companies to meet these metrics.

For all of our successes in business or other careers, why is it that conversations about money still intimidate so many of us women? Female entrepreneurs get a bad rap for not "owning" their numbers and financials with as much confidence as their male counterparts. Women investors' eyes often glaze over when angel investing courses turn to understanding cap tables, determining company valuation, or assessing a proforma company spreadsheet. I have always shied away from deep financial analysis and had a lack of confidence in my ability to assess a strong investment opportunity once the discussion turns to the economics of a deal. That has changed as I have become a more active angel investor and had to take a crash course in finance as a fund manager. Luckily, I also have had several very competent and confident numbers junkies at my back running our fund, so no one has to ultimately rely on my math or spreadsheet skills.

But understanding the basic economics of a deal as well as what to look for at a high level in a company's financials is worth spending time learning. Many introductory angel investing courses can get you quickly up to speed on valuations, cap tables, and understanding the fundamentals of revenues and expenditures that lead to early stage company growth and success. While it does not take an MBA or financial certification to be an impactful and successful angel investor, it will only help you and the companies you invest in if you ground yourself in the financial basics, ideally alongside others with experience in angel investing.

Invest in the Change You Want to See in the World

If you are a woman interested in expanding your knowledge about money and how to control and feel good about what you own, consider joining an investment circle such as Invest for Better (IFB). The IFB program challenges you to think more deeply about your relationship with money and where and how it is invested. IFB has created a network of women exploring their own investment strategies and aligning their investments with their personal values with frequent sessions led by women practicing and leading alternative investment opportunities. The companion book, *Activate Your Money* by Janine Firpo is also a great place to start as you explore new ways to think about the potential impact of your investments.

Another way to begin expanding your investment knowledge alongside other women is to join a women-led angel group or network. Golden Seeds, The New Table, Astia or one of many other emerging networks or funds built by women for women are places to start, which offer safe places to ask questions and dip your toe in. Don't let your feelings about money or your own confidence in your financial acumen get in the way of becoming an angel investor.

Much like any industry, angel investing has its own set of jargon and commonly held practices that are not difficult once you chart a course to understand them. The next Act in this book outlines how we learned about structuring and raising our first angel fund. Our JumpFund general partners spent a year diving deep into angel investor training with Golden Seeds and then many more years learning from deeply experienced angels with the Angel Capital Association (ACA), the largest professional network of angel investors in the world. Courses from understanding basic company valuation and term sheets to more advanced courses on cap tables and exit strategies can be taken over time as you find your angel wings. I've also included a glossary in the appendix which covers some of the basic terminology of early stage investing.

You don't have to like numbers or finance to become an angel investor, as I have successfully proven. You just need the passion and interest in moving your money to more directly align with your values and how you want it to positively impact others as they launch their own dreams. Invest in the change you want to see in the world. Invest for better.

ACT IV

A Woman's Guide to Angel Investing

4

A Woman's Guide to Angel Investing

If we want to see change in the world, we need to create it, invest in it, be it!

—Marcia Dawood, Host, The Angel Next Door

Earning Your Angel Wings

Since launching JumpFund over ten years ago, many women have come to me or my partners to learn about how we got started. They often have intentions of building their own funds or networks in their communities as they have discovered the same pain points for female founders which JumpFund has witnessed—market bias, lack of access to capital, or limited support systems. I am always thrilled when I find like-minded women looking to jump into angel investing or start their own angel community and try to give them real, practical advice to understand all that goes into starting and running a successful early stage investment group.

I often start with the basics to be sure they are serious. First, this is NOT charity or philanthropy, the intention should be investing for strong returns. Second, this is NOT a side hustle, building a fund or network takes significant time and effort to do well. And third, it takes money to make money—management fees or membership dues often do not cover all of the legal, accounting, and administrative work that is required to both start and manage an early stage investing partnership. The standard now is a minimum $20M fund (versus our baby $2.5M first fund) to allow enough resources to cover management and administrative costs and write meaningful checks. The following provides the basic "block and tackling" of building your own angel group but is particularly geared towards women wanting to start something by and for other women. *Note: key terms related to angel investing are bolded in this section and a full glossary of terms relevant to first-time angel investors has been included at the end of this book for reference.*

What does it mean to be an "angel" investor? There is a mythology around those individuals who invest their own money in other people's startup ventures. These elusive investors sit in their ivory towers, shrouded in mystery, doling out cash to hungry entrepreneurs at whim. They meet founders in bars or coffee shops where "back of the napkin" deals take place. They are fickle and capricious, and it seems difficult to understand what they "really want" and how to best pitch a company concept to them.

For some women entrepreneurs, angel investors are also seen as predators, lurking and waiting to pounce on insecurity and doubt, and often wanting a personal favor in return. As highlighted previously, there have been cases of male investors who comment on female founders' physical attractiveness or the clothes they are wearing during their pitch, instead of pertinent questions about their company. Others have been known, under the guise of potential investment, to invite women to dinner or in some cases their homes or hotel rooms to "discuss business." These predatory investors hold the purse strings and thus the power to make or break your nascent venture. If this happens to you, run, don't walk from these types of investors. And tell your story. Call them out and stop these insidious practices.

But as the landscape of early stage investors is beginning to change, so is who we are and our motives. Most of the angel investors I work with, both male and female, have at their core a desire to help. They have accumulated their own significant wealth and resources, either from building their own successful businesses or inherited from others who have done so, and have a desire to "pay it forward" while also seeking a return on their investment. Angel investing is not charity, which it is often confused with—the money is expected to come back to the investor, ideally with significant gains for all. However it is based on faith and a fundamental belief that this particular entrepreneur and the company they are building have what it takes to be successful.

My angel investment journey began with a desire to level the playing field for women entrepreneurs. I was willing to devote my time, talent, and treasure to the cause and was able to rally like-minded women around me who understood the need to use our personal resources to make a difference for women starting their own businesses who may not have the same access to early stage funding as their male counterparts. My passion also stemmed from my lifelong pursuit of equity in all sectors of our society, particularly in education and ultimately economic parity. Much like the question of why some children have access to quality education while others do not, why should it be that a sector of our society should have access to capital to build their businesses while others atrophy by their lack of early stage resources?

So, how does one begin their journey as an angel investor? First, it is important that you assess your own personal wealth and determine if you can take on the significant risk of investing in early stage companies. Whether investing directly in a company or an early stage investment fund, you must at minimum meet the **accredited investor**[22] thresholds which are currently $1mm in personal net worth and/or $200,000 annual income ($300,000 joint marital income).[23] While the SEC (Securities and Exchange Commission) has expanded the definition to also include "professional knowledge" as a fund administrator or financial advisor, the rules are meant to protect investors from the potential risks of losing all of one's investment in private placements not necessarily governed by the SEC.

Crowdfunding, where a company solicits either direct donations or equity investment via public platforms such as We Funder or Our Crowd, is a newer model of raising capital in which investors do not always need to meet accredited investor requirements. Yet, these investments also come with higher levels of risk and very few safeguards for investors and should still be considered as a small portion of one's overall investment strategy. Some angel investors utilize a wide range of investment vehicles to access deals and invest in companies that interest them—from large deal-sharing platforms such as Angel List to any number of angel investment funds, groups, and networks. Once you understand the early stage investment landscape, you can choose which vehicle and risk profile is best suited for you.

Once you've determined that you are accredited and are willing to carve out some portion of your investment portfolio for higher risk, but potentially higher reward opportunities, the next step is to develop your acumen to make well-reasoned investments. There are many ways to test the waters of angel investing in a relatively safe and supportive environment.

First, seek further education on becoming an angel investor. As mentioned previously, the Angel Capital Association (ACA) is the vanguard of angel education and resources for early stage investors, from their Angel University to a wide variety of affinity groups, networks, and funds that are members of this well-established organization. As an individual or member of an angel group, you can access training on everything from **term sheets** and

due diligence to advanced **cap tables,** both in person or through ACA's library of online offerings.

Second, find a fund or network in your own community or region with a group of like-minded individuals collectively making investments. Some angel groups are industry sector focused while others, like JumpFund, may direct their investments towards underrepresented founders or social impact companies. Many also offer their own angel education programs, such as Angela Lee's 37 Angels in New York or Portfolia's collection of funds comprised of all female investors investing in specific verticals such as "Active Aging" or "FemTech." Still, others like Harlem Capital or GoldenSeeds offer full "angel investor 101" or "boot camp" courses as part of their membership process.

As a new angel investor, it is important to gain deeper knowledge of this unique asset class. Early stage investing often means establishing a relationship with and funding a company from a nascent stage in its development. That means there may be little to no financials to track, customer success to monitor, or products fully developed. Angels often lean on qualitative versus quantitative data to determine the likelihood of success, such as the founder's sector experience, market and competitor analysis, and a compelling business plan. For this reason, learning from other angel investors who have been building successful portfolios of young companies is key to becoming a successful angel yourself.

Most introductory angel investment courses will cover the "basics." These include but are not limited to: conducting effective early stage company due diligence, understanding company **valuations** and deal terms, reviewing term sheets and different types of startup funding structures (**preferred equity, convertible notes, SAFES,** etc), investor roles and responsibilities (including serving on a startup's board of directors), and potential **exit strategies.**

Some angel groups have clearly defined **investment theses** while others help you define your own personal goals and objectives, whether it is based on your experience in a particular industry or your interest in an area of impact, such as gender lens investing or the environment.

While I always say that angel investing is not "rocket science," it does require diligence, time, personal resources, and a terrific amount of patience to do it well. A common rule of thumb in angel investing is that as an individual you should aim to build a portfolio of at least ten companies investing anywhere between 10-15% percent of your total assets to mitigate the risk of these volatile investments. early stage investors can expect that at least a third or more of the companies they invest in will fail, some may return a portion of their initial investment, and only a few (maybe even one or two!) may provide significant returns, generally in the ballpark of 3-10x the initial investment.[24] In fact, only one company's success may be the one to carry the **ROI** (return on investment) of your entire angel investment portfolio.

Values Alignment

As an angel investor, you should consider the impact you want your investments to make and the reason behind why you choose to take this risk with your own capital. Before JumpFund partners ever went out and recruited investors, we had to establish our own "why." What was our mission? How would we convey that message to potential investors? What did we fundamentally care about in this work? What was our BHAG, our big hairy audacious goal?

While our initial messaging was centered on the importance of access to capital for women entrepreneurs, it became clear early on that investors saw this as a philanthropic endeavor, not one related to their personal investments. Thus, we went back to the drawing board and revamped our pitch to be laser-focused on investment return potential and the arbitrage opportunity our particular investment thesis represented. We knew from our own experiences that women were both highly capable and highly successful at starting and running their own businesses. We also knew that our group of women partners had unique expertise to bring to bear on selecting and adding value to early stage companies in which to invest. And, we had been conducting research that proved companies with women's leadership resulted in better returns.

From this research and trial and error, we developed a mission statement we felt captured our dual goals:

To invest women's capital in female-led companies with growth potential to generate a strong financial return and elevate the role of women in business.

We also established guiding values to help center our work and provide direction and purpose:

→ We value *entrepreneurs* who are making the incredible leap to start their own companies
→ We value our *investors* who support our mission and vision
→ We value *access to capital for all* entrepreneurs and *gender diversity* on start-up teams.
→ We are committed to *investment discipline* and *due diligence* in our practices.
→ We strive to build *supportive networks* and opportunities for *collaboration*
→ We want to continually "pay it forward" by *mentoring and coaching* other women.

Finally, our ultimate vision (BHAG) has been **to establish the Southeast as the BEST place for a woman to invest in or start a business.**

I am proud that we have held true to our mission, vision, and values and have begun to see our impact over the past ten years. Even with our small dollars, we have helped change the landscape for female founders and women as angel investors. Other angel investors and even venture capitalists are learning from our example as they scramble to diversify their portfolios after so many years of being publicly shamed for investing primarily in white, male-led teams. We can now point to a myriad of women-led companies, with early dollars from female-led firms and investors, who have successfully grown and profitably exited their companies despite the headwinds of gender bias, less access to capital, and sexual harassment across the startup landscape.

Angel Fund Basics

In the early days of our first fund, given that we didn't know what we didn't yet know, JumpFund took the advice of other fund managers we trusted to formulate the basic structure of our first fund. Venture capital funds come in many flavors and forms, but the most common is a "2 and 20" model—meaning a 2% **management fee** and 20% carry to the general partnership (GP), which manages the fund. The **carry** refers to the percentage of profits, after returning investors' initial capital, that the GP realizes for its role should the fund be successful. Within that basic structure, we had to decide how to price individual investor **shares** or units within our fund, which for us landed at $30k per share for our first fund and $50k per share for JumpFund II. We felt it was important to set a reasonable bar for first-time, female investors who did not have other experience with early stage private equity funds, which often command a minimum investment of $250k per share or higher.

When an investor or **limited partner** commits capital to the fund, it is commonly called over a time frame known as the "investment period." There may be an initial **capital call**, such as 15-20% to seed the fund, then subsequent calls of 5-20% annually depending on investment opportunities and how quickly the GP can deploy the capital. So, if you commit $50,000 to an angel fund, you might be asked to put in $10,000 at signing, and then an additional $5-10,000 annually until your commitment is fully funded. It is good to get a sense on the front end as to expectations for these capital calls—how frequent, the percentage of your total commitment expected annually, and timing to help you plan accordingly.

Fund management, when the bulk of the work is done on a voluntary basis, with no returns or carry expected for years to come, can make it difficult to determine roles, responsibilities, and equity compensation for members of the general partner. Establishing our first fund, we also had to decide how to divide our partnership equitably and fairly, given that everyone but the **managing partner** (me) had other full-time jobs. The JumpFund decided that since I was devoting my full time and energy to managing the fund, my equity ownership in the GP would be larger than the other six partners, which means that I would receive more of the "carry" or payback when and if our fund is successful, a strong incentive to do well.

Over time we have also helped compensate the GP for its tax burden on internal capital gains and covered travel and other associated fund expenses to the extent possible. With limited management fees, we do not have the ability to compensate ourselves directly for our work. Instead, we use our lean budget to support a part-time, paid fund administrator and other outside resources to help with accounting, financial management, investor communications, and essential aspects of fund management.

Our second fund had a slightly different GP structure, losing one original member and adding two additional partners, so we had to adjust accordingly. Just like any business, leadership often changes over time and we had to adjust to accommodate the exit of partners who wanted to move on and new partners who were eager to join our management team. Having good legal counsel and well-written formation documents for both the management group (LLC) as well as the limited partnership (LP) you will form when starting a fund will save you many headaches down the road. To learn more about fund structure and management, I suggest you explore the Angel Capital Association's "Angel Box," an A to Z guide that covers the basics of getting a new angel investor group or fund off the ground.[25]

Other small angel funds such as ours have explored alternative structures and methods to manage and compensate their GPs. Next Wave Impact Fund, used an "investment committee" instead of a general partner structure, in which the fund decision-makers are compensated with an additional carry from investments on which they led due diligence and/or companies for which they serve as liaisons or board members. Other funds may have a smaller number of partners in their GP or even solo managing partners, which makes it easier to compensate their work with the limited management fees garnered by funds of less than $20M. Fearless Fund, mentioned earlier in this book, has also augmented its management fees with grants that help fund its operations and staff including its managing partners.

Another consideration is the lifespan of your fund. Most funds have a "vintage" which indicates a closed fund with a specific time stamp on when they stopped taking on new limited partners—either because they hit their fundraising goal (or were unable to) or want to cap the number of investors and thus ownership dilution in the fund. Closed-end funds have a typical life span of ten years (3-5 years of investment period, 7-10 years to "harvest") often with two one-year extensions (or more) depending on how long it takes to exit or disentangle from all its investments. As an investor in a fund, you should plan on your capital being tied up for a long period of time and highly illiquid. There are also fund structures that are "evergreen" where funds are continually being raised, but these require a very different structure for accounting and tracking both investments and returns.

Ultimately, find a good lawyer with experience in fund structures and/or limited partnerships. It is also good to find accountants early on who understand the complexities of LLC/LP structures and how they interrelate. Other startup funds are also often happy to share their documents as examples and the Angel Capital Association has a full library of resources to help guide you on fund and/or angel network structures. This is definitely a place where you do not need to recreate the wheel and can lean on the experience of others to get started.

Key Decisions to Consider When Structuring an Angel Fund

What price per unit/share is the sweet spot for your target market? Women who have not had previous angel investing or private funds experience are less likely to make six-figure commitments out of the gate.

How much do you need to manage your fund? Is the typical 2/20 structure enough to cover your expenses? Will you need to consider raising operations support outside of your LP commitments to fund operations? Do your managing partners expect compensation or are they willing to work for the carry?

What is the projected lifespan of your fund? Typical funds have a ten-year term with two or more optional years by vote of the partnership, if necessary,

---

to extend the fund's life in order to maximize returns. Angel investing is patient capital, so consider how long your investors will be willing to commit as well as how quickly you can deploy capital into companies with clear and compelling exit strategies.

How long is your investment period? Given that fund life spans are only ten+ years you need to deploy capital within the first several years of your fund in order to capitalize on the average trajectory of start-up businesses, most of which need a minimum of 3-5 years to percolate. A common investment period, in which your fund would make both its initial and any follow-on investments, is five years which gives you an additional five years to work towards company exits and returns for your investors.

What are your plans if there are changes to the general partner/founding team? Life happens and sometimes people need to get out of big commitments they have made, leaving room for new folks to join the team. No matter if you are a two person or ten person partnership, make sure your documents support the "marriage and divorce" aspects of any good business relationship and that all partners understand that this is a long-term commitment of their time, talent, and resources.

Recruiting Investors

Fundraising for your first angel fund is akin to an entrepreneur raising her own round of investment capital. You must prove that what you are building is worth the investment and that investors understand this is an illiquid, long-term commitment, hopefully worth the wait. Because many women may be starting their first funds, they have the disadvantage of being a first-time fund manager with no track record and most potential investors meeting you for the first-time. In addition, we continue to face market biases as female-led funds are not as prevalent and gender discrimination exists in the financial world just as it does on the entrepreneurial playing field.

For our first fund, JumpFund founders started with who we knew and might trust us to launch this endeavor, given our collective track records in business, finance, and philanthropy. Each of our general partners dug deep into their personal and professional rolodexes and recruited those they knew to be 1) accredited investors 2) women who had been in business or professional services who might understand the pain points of female entrepreneurs, OR 3) had engaged in philanthropic causes supporting women and girls in our community. Although the concept was new—most women in our community had not considered direct investments in early stage companies, particularly those that were women-led. Our mission to engage women's capital to invest in women resonated with many of these successful female leaders to whom we pitched our bold, new idea.

Much like any entrepreneur seeking funding, we had to develop an investor pitch deck and supporting materials to show how we as first-time women in venture capital investing in underrepresented founders were going to pull this off. Our early pitches had a strong focus on our mission and vision and why investing in women-led ventures was so critically important. Those presentations resonated with the philanthropists in the room, but we found a broader, deeper audience when we shifted our pitch to focus on the investment returns potential of our fund. Our premise became one of "arbitrage"—if women are starting businesses at high rates, have proven high potential for success, yet are not receiving adequate funding to grow and scale, there is a gap in the market we intended to fill.

This second pitch proved much more successful, especially with women who had business acumen and had experiences of their own with bias and glass ceilings. As with any investor pool you tap, there will always be those who get it and are drawn to your vision and those who don't or for whom the timing is just not right. We also surprisingly found a minority of women who felt that other women did not need "special treatment" or funding targeted just for them as they had bootstrapped their own companies and clawed their way up the ladder without assistance themselves. If they could do it, so could other women.

While women with this perspective were few and far between, they also could have been amazing allies. This line of thinking frustrated us as we knew the statistics and felt strongly that investing specifically in women-led ventures was paramount given the huge gaps in access to capital. Although we didn't think this of all those who rejected us, we did internally repeat Madeline Albright's wise words: "There's a special place in hell for women who do not support other women." As women, we need to rally our resources to combat the inequities, bias, and roadblocks that we face at every turn, be that in business, finance, or society at large.

Within six months, we had raised our first fund, landing on $2.5M as our target size with investment from over fifty local women as well as one corporate and foundation investment. We have always been extremely proud that we stuck to our original intent with our first fund and recruited only women as investors, proving that there were "women like us" who saw the opportunity to activate their capital to support other women. The women we attracted to take a risk on our first fund spanned age and professions, from bankers, marketing professionals, and finance executives to artists, philanthropists, and university professors. And the majority of these first investors came from our own, small community in Chattanooga which demonstrated this could be done almost anywhere. We also garnered a few institutional investors, including the startup bank in which our partner Stefanie had been involved, as well as a local foundation with a mission to support our city's entrepreneurial ecosystem.

Raising funding for first-time, "emerging" fund managers is often difficult. It is especially so if you are a woman and/or person of color, as you confront many of the same biases and challenges that female or BIPOC founders face. Track record is heavily weighted in this business, so without that it is difficult to get investors to take a risk on your first fund. The more you can build a team with experience amongst your general partnership or leadership team, especially those with investment or finance expertise and/or successful entrepreneurial exits, the better. When we launched our first fund we engaged several outside advisors, including men who had started other funds, to add the cache of expertise and stamp of approval to our efforts.

All of the female fund managers I spoke with for this book have experienced setbacks raising their first funds, and some even when raising their second fund. The Jump-Fund started with a very small goal of $2.5M for its first fund and with the combined networks of our founding partners, were quickly able to raise that capital from mostly women in our own backyard. True Wealth Ventures, run by Sara Brand and Kerry Rupp in Houston, talk about how it took them two and a half years to raise their first fund, which had a goal of $20M but stagnated at its first $10M until the very end of their fund closing when they were able to finally reel in another $9M in commitments. According to Sara, 50-70% of all first-time funds fail to raise their full targets and many only reach half the goal of what they set out to raise.

Mindshift Capital is another female-led fund, run by my former Next Wave colleagues Heather Henyon and Marcia Dawood, which also struggled to meet its fundraising goal. They planned to raise a $50M+ global fund targeting women-led companies in the U.S. and MENA (Middle East/North Africa) region, with Heather's deep ties in Dubai where she was involved with a women's entrepreneurship support network (WOMENA). According to Marcia, part of their pitch ended up being their Achilles heel as potential investors were skittish about making cross-border investments, even though all of the investments and tax implications were handled by the fund, using the Cayman Islands as neutral banking territory.

Marcia and Heather also found that the network of women they thought would be interested in their proposition to invest with a global gender lens, would express interest but then walk away when it came time to write a check. And like many of us women raising our first funds, the two felt major bias from institutional and male investors who did not "get" their investment thesis or did not feel that these two women, although extremely well-versed in early stage investing with long, successful track records and extensive personal angel investment portfolios, were up to the task of running a venture fund. In the end, they closed Mindshift's first fund at around $10M, far shy of their initial lofty goal.

Fearless Fund (originally called the Women of Color Collective) struggled to raise its first $5M for their Atlanta-based fund focused on women of color. Co-founders Arian Simone and Keisha Knight Pulliam (child star Rudy on the Cosby Show) had extensive networks and huge PR pull, but no direct fund management experience which combined with being women of color starting their first fund, proved to be a triple whammy. We saw a reflection of JumpFund's early efforts in what Arian and her team were building and became an early investor and mentor in Fearless Fund, helping share formation documents, legal counsel, and fund management advising. Yet, it wasn't until large financial institutions such as Bank of America, Allied Bank, JP Morgan, and even PayPal were challenged to expand funding for BIPOC founders at the height of the Black Lives Matter Movement, that Fearless experienced a boost to their fundraising efforts. In less than a year, they had attracted investment from these financial giants, expanding their fund to $25.8M. This expanded fund size allowed them to build out their team and increase the number and size of their investments, which have now grown to more than thirty companies led by women of color.

Common knowledge amongst early stage fund managers is that you need to raise a minimum $20M fund to cover your basic costs. With the standard 2% management fee on a fund less than $20M it is difficult to pay a full-time team for fund management, let alone the managing partners themselves. Thus most GPs of smaller funds such as ours must work hard to achieve outsized returns for their funds so that they can be compensated with the 20% carry if the fund is profitable.

Many smaller funds have turned to new fund management platforms to streamline their back-office support and reduce overhead. CARTA and SERAF are two such platforms used by emerging fund managers as portals for fund accounting, investor communications, and tracking of potential returns as well as exits. CARTA is also commonly used by sophisticated startups for cap table management and investor relations, with its two-sided portal for both entrepreneurs and fund managers.

Even with $20M it is often a struggle to support a full time team, as the Fearless fund has found. With the influx of new investment, they were able to expand their team to a total of ten staff, including an investment analyst but have also had to find outside support for their operations through grants. The JumpFund, with our relatively smaller capital raise of just under $8M, has had to rely on the support of a family office and only supports one, part-time fund administrator.

As with many smaller, almost all volunteer first-time funds, our general partners all "work for the carry" which means we reap the rewards of a highly successful portfolio of companies when they have successful exits. This is particularly true with women-led fund management, where limited partner check sizes are smaller. Women frankly don't often write six-figure checks in this asset class where most male-led funds expect an initial $250k commitment. Comparatively, the gender lens funds I've been involved with generally start at minimum investments of $30-50k per share. Until we can more fully prove out the strong IRR of gender lens funds and more women rise up the ranks as fund managers, we will continue to face the same challenges to raising funding as our female founders.

Female Founder Pipeline

As the only fund solely dedicated to financing women-led ventures in the Southeast back in 2014, we had as much opportunity as we could manage. I like to say that we planted our JumpFund flag and it was akin to opening the floodgates, the demand was so great. Women had come to expect they could not find capital, whether it was debt, angel, or venture, to grow their business so they had taken to bootstrapping their companies, seeking grant funding, or hopping into one business accelerator program after another to keep the lights on. When we started our first small fund, you would have thought we were an oasis in the desert the way we had companies reaching out for potential funding.

To manage this flow, we quickly set up a system to receive and review applications online. Golden Seeds had piloted a new deal flow management platform, ProSeeder, which at the time they had helped specifically design for use with angel investing networks such as ours. This platform allowed us to send companies to a portal where they could provide us with basic information about their company, answer intake questions about their business, and upload a pitch deck, business plan, or other supporting documents. It also allowed all of our JumpFund partners to review applications in a single place and even had a ranking system built in to rate their interest in companies we wanted to learn more about. And since Golden Seeds had helped launch the platform, it became an effective way for other angel investing groups to share deals easily across our networks. While ProSeeder is no longer in business, other platforms have emerged to help with deal flow management, including Dealum or Seraf.

Another way we sourced deals early on was to collaborate with regional accelerator programs. StartCo, an accelerator in Memphis, TN was launching a program targeting only women as they had had trouble diversifying their accelerator cohorts and decided they needed to address common barriers they had seen women entrepreneurs experience. This new program, called UpStart, recruited a young, serial entrepreneur from the West Coast as its director who herself had experienced many of the pain points facing female entrepreneurs. As Upstart recruited companies to Memphis from across the country, Jump-Fund looked at this as an opportunity to expand its reach and support another effort focused solely on women.

For the first two years of our fund, we collaborated with Upstart, vetting the companies they were bringing in, providing mentoring and advisory support, and partnering with their other funders to make early, seed investments in hopes that these women-led ventures would stay and grow in the Southeast. For us, this allowed us to get in early with several companies now in our portfolio—including Sweetbio, developing manuka honey-infused wound healing products, and DevCon Detect (now Otto), providing client-side cybersecurity—but with a lower initial amount of funding and thus less risk.

One of the unique tenets of UpStart was that it was designed to be a "reverse" accelerator program. Mara Lewis, who ran the program for several years and helped develop the initial curriculum, had seen women leave early stage venture programs or not even apply due to the competitive, "bro" culture seen in traditional startup accelerators. She thought, "Why don't we flip this narrative on its head and start with a more nurturing and collaborative environment that builds up companies instead of immediately breaking them down only to rebuild them better and stronger?" This psychology seemed to work well for Upstart, as women who were reticent to share their "babies" (company ideas) for fear of being told they were ugly or not going to succeed, could instead explore what it takes to successfully build a business within a supportive program that was wholly dedicated to their success. Their baby might have a few growing pains or look a bit different in the end, but it was not a demoralizing or demeaning process to get there.

Through the Upstart accelerator, we were involved in choosing companies to participate and ended up investing $15-25K of seed capital in five of them upon completion of the program. Several experienced early success but fizzled after a few years as they struggled to find their footing. Others continued to grow and even stayed in Memphis or the greater Southeast as they found a supportive ecosystem of business partners and funders.

If you are looking for deal flow of promising companies, I would encourage you to work with accelerators in your own state or region to source deals. Having come through an accelerator program, companies have often been pre-vetted and asked many of the questions early stage investors will pose in due diligence, thus they are better prepared with answers and have thought through problems at an earlier stage. Working with an accelerator, you can lean-in as a mentor, host office hours—as Jump-Fund did at Chattanooga's Company Lab accelerator for several years—or attend demo days to listen to pitches of companies that have come through these programs, tuned up and ready to launch or expand.

As gender lens investors, we also had leverage to push regional accelerator programs to be more critical about diversity in their cohorts. As mentioned before, both our local and state-level pitch events were woefully lacking in either women or people of color. With the establishment of JumpFund, we were able to further press to see a wider diversity of founders on these stages with high potential for investment. LaunchTN, our statewide umbrella organization for early stage capital and innovation, quickly rose to the challenge after our initial conversations, and within a year there were several women pitching, two in which we invested.

The first was Jewel Burks, originally from a small rural town in Tennessee and founder of Partpic, a parts visualization platform, which provided our fund's first successful exit. Another was Lucy Beard, co-founder of 3D printed custom shoe company Feetz, which had been recruited through the GigTank's program at the Company Lab (Co. Lab) and went on to pitch at Launch TN's annual pitch event. Along with LaunchTN, the Co.Lab in Chattanooga also started intentionally recruiting more women and people of color to its accelerator programs and by 2020 more than fifty percent of all companies they served were led by women and at least a third by entrepreneurs of color.

Beyond accelerators, building up a network of trusted

co-investors is another key to successful deal sourcing. Our first fund had very few other co-investors in our regional sandbox, as no other Southeast fund or network was yet focused on investing in women and very few of the male-led funds had invested in even a single female founder. As we became more involved in the Angel Capital Association and met other women starting funds and networks, we began to create our own club, trading deals and co-investing our relatively smaller dollars for greater impact.

Through the ACA, a group of us launched the Growing Women's Capital network of women investing in women. We also joined the ACA's Southeast investor network as well as a newly formed Impact Investing group, which gave us a platform to elevate women-led companies on these investors' radars. Many investors have FOMO (fear of missing out) and once another investor or two has put money into a deal, there are likely others who will more easily follow, especially if there has been good due diligence performed on the company. It is an easier path once a company has gone through the diligence process with another investor group as their findings can be shared and less work has to be done to close a deal.

As a smaller fund with limited internal resources, we found that by co-investing with trusted partners such as Golden Seeds, Next Wave, or well-known Southeast investor networks such as Venture South or Innova, we could more quickly decide on an investment than if we led a deal and conducted all of the rigorous diligence ourselves. Building trusted relationships with these early stage investor groups also allowed JumpFund to showcase companies in which we've invested to a wider audience of like-minded investors, many of whom have co-invested in our portfolio companies.

While it is important to see many deals, some even say

hundreds of deals, at the top of your deal flow "funnel" in order to get to the handful you might eventually invest in, you can cut through the noise faster if you partner with others to find strong companies. In the past ten years we have looked at hundreds of companies, whittling them down through our application and screening process, then pitch review and due diligence, and ultimately, a very few to actual funding. Below is a chart of all deals that came through our process from 2014-2018 and the number that actually made it to funding, which was relatively high at the time as we were in our most active deal sourcing and investment period of both funds.

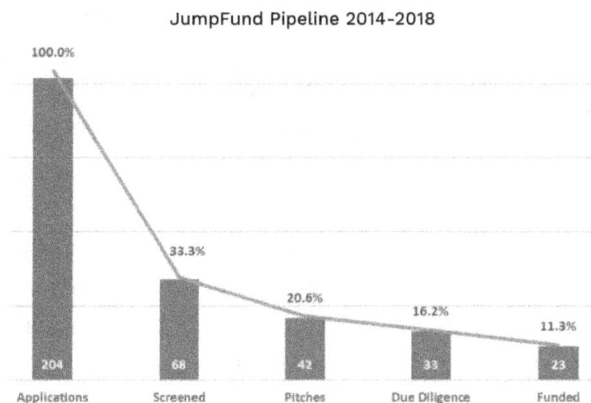

JumpFund Pipeline 2014-2018

As you can see, less than a third of applications even make it to the first screening, generally because they did not meet basic criteria: women's leadership/ownership, scalability, product/market fit, or inadequate financial projections or business plans. Screening duties were shared amongst the general partners and our fund administrator, and generally consisted of a call with the founder to learn more about their company and if they were a right fit for our fund. We did not invite companies to pitch or move them to diligence unless they had a high likelihood of making it through our process. Although we have seen many more companies over the lifespan of our two funds, the following provides a snapshot of how we moved them through our pipeline and into the Dolphin Tank.

The Dolphin Tank

From the beginning, we started to refer to our pitch meetings with entrepreneurs as the Dolphin Tank. When we started JumpFund, Shark Tank was a primetime TV mainstay and most people knew the basic lingo of venture capital speak and the way the judges are always trying to one-up each other with tough, sometimes inane questions and terrible "sharky" deal offers, designed to trip up entrepreneurs and of course, make good TV. Our process was intentionally different. We wanted to be more open and transparent both about what it took to get to a pitch with us as well as what would happen afterward.

When making early stage investments, you want to see as many deals as possible at the top of the funnel and be able to get to yes or no decisions fairly quickly at each stage of the process so as not to drag things out for the busy entrepreneur. While we admit ours was not a perfect process, we quickly determined that we needed clear criteria upfront and a rating system to more fairly and efficiently decide on who we would like to hear a pitch from. Mirroring our intake application to Golden Seeds, we were able to more quickly vet deals based on a set of basic criteria the entrepreneur was asked to provide, including:

→ **Business Summary**—a brief paragraph similar to an "elevator pitch"
→ **Founder and C-suite Ownership**—confirmation that the company is woman-led

→ **Problem and Solution**—what are they trying to solve? What is their unique solution?

→ **Business Model**—product/service, clients, sources of revenue, pricing, costs, etc

→ **Management Team**—background, experience, advisors, connections

→ **Market Opportunity**—target market, size of the total addressable market (TAM), and potential market share

→ **Customers**—who are they and why would they pay?

→ **Sales and Marketing**—what is it going to take to get people to buy? How can you retain/grow customers? What is your go-to-market strategy?

→ **Competition**—who are your competitors and what differentiates your company?

→ **Exit Strategy**—how are you going to make money for your investors?

→ **Deal Information**—fundraising goal, estimated pre-money valuation, terms of the deal

→ **Company Stage**—based on revenues and traction (early, seed, growth, later)

→ **Financials**—current revenue, P&L, 5 year projections detailing scalability

To review deals on the platform, our general partner team, which made all the investment decisions for both funds, met for the first several years on a bi-monthly basis. Each month we would rate and review applications that met our fundamentals—women's ownership, Southeast-based, compelling problem/solution, competitive advantage, growth potential to a minimum of $20M in annual recurring revenue (ARR) in five years and a clear path to exit. Those who rose to the top and received the most votes from all of the partners would move on to a telephone screening round before being invited to pitch. If we had seen the company at another pitch event or the entrepreneur had been referred to us by another fund we respected, the company might move more quickly to a pitch.

Until March 2020 all of our company pitches were in person. Since the pandemic, it is now normalized to make investment decisions based solely on a video pitch. This was actually the process Next Wave Impact Fund used even pre-pandemic with limited partners spread out across the country and has become a more efficient and democratic way for founders to get a first crack at potential investors. Since our fund focused on companies in the Southeast and a key piece of our criteria was getting to know the entrepreneurs to determine if they were a fit for our funding, we preferred to only have in-person pitches. Depending on the travel necessary to make the pitch, we sometimes offered to put the entrepreneur up overnight as getting to Chattanooga is not always easy. We also would try to spend additional time with entrepreneurs making the trek, either taking them to lunch to debrief afterward or meeting for coffee beforehand, to get to know them better.

Although entrepreneurs were still nervous walking into a pitch with us, as they would with any potential investors, we often received feedback that meeting with us was "different" and "refreshing" for these women founders working hard to raise capital for their ventures. We tried to make it a safe space for them to ask questions of us to see if we were a right fit for them and tailored our questions to be more promotional vs. prevention-oriented. As women investing in women, we wanted to consciously shift the paradigm and allow female founders the advantage of pitching their companies in a positive, growth-focused light as their male counterparts were normally afforded.

During the pitch our partner team would use our expertise, whether in tech, finance, real estate, or management, to lean into specific aspects of the business models presented. Yet, we never presumed that the woman standing in front of us was not worthy of selling her company to us.

Whether she was the CEO, COO, or the tech wizard of the company, we expected her to know her shit. Her company needed to be her baby, yet we never questioned if she had "other" children or was planning to have any as is often the case for female entrepreneurs. As mothers ourselves, we are exceptionally proud of the many mommas in our JumpFund portfolio family, most of whom had their first or even fourth babies while running their startups.

The best pitches are always brief (no more than 10 minutes) and comprise a select group of slides (7-10) that highlight specific aspects investors are most interested in and leave us wanting to know more. Similar to most early stage venture investors, the basics JumpFund expects to see in a business pitch include:

→ **Product**—Define the problem and solution—Why are you building this? Who is the audience? Why would they buy it/use it?

→ **Market**—How big is it? What fraction do you expect to command?

→ **Revenue**—How do you plan to make money? What are the economics (margins, COGs, etc)? How would you scale to a minimum $20M company in 3-5 years?

→ **Competition**—Who are your competitors? What differentiates your product/service? How can you do it faster/better?

→ **Special sauce**—Is or can any aspect of the business be protected (IP)? If not, what makes your company unique and how can you keep others from taking your idea/market share?

→ **People**—Who is on your team and who else do you need to help you scale? Who are your advisors and/or board members? What are your qualifications as founder/CEO?

→ **Raise**—How much capital do you need now and in the future to grow your business? What is your company's valuation? What are the deal terms (if established)? Who else has invested in this round or past rounds?

One of our most important questions to founders was always why they wanted JumpFund as an investor. As a small fund focused on female founders in the Southeast, we wanted to know what they felt JumpFund might bring to the table beyond our minimal dollars. We rarely, if ever, "lead" an investment (put the most money in and set the terms) so there had to be strong reasons why they would want us as investors. Many times it was that they wanted to have more women involved in building their company and on their cap tables—which often also helps with establishing and keeping woman-owned business status (retaining 51%+ women's ownership of your business, including investors).[26] Some founders, who had done their homework, saw the skills and expertise JumpFund had to offer from its partners and investor network and they wanted to tap in. Still others understood the growing power of our network and that we had access to other gender lens investors who might also come alongside us if we chose to invest.

Once the founder's ten-minute pitch with twenty minutes of Q&A was complete, our partners would debrief and make a decision about moving forward with due diligence, or a deeper review of the company. Initial diligence could be a follow-up phone call or email with additional questions that arose after the pitch. Or, we might feel strongly enough about what we heard and had a good enough sense from our in-person meeting with the founder that this was a relationship we wanted to explore further. If you think of the pitch as the first date, moving to due diligence is akin to deciding you want to spend more time with that person to get to know them better.

As we like to say, a term sheet for an investment in a company is like a prenuptial agreement—we are going to be married for a time and then our relationship will ideally end in a tidy, mutually agreeable divorce (or a slightly messier one with both sides protected if it doesn't). Thus in due diligence, everything needs to be on the table. We begin with a standard diligence checklist that covers documents pertaining to all aspects of the business, from financials to marketing plans.

This part of the process can be slow if the entrepreneur does not already have these materials at hand so I highly recommend that entrepreneurs gather these in advance, collect them in an easily accessible online platform such as Dropbox, and be able to turn them over to the potential investor asap. We never signed NDAs (non disclosure agreements) as part of our process and most early stage investors will not since we constantly review companies that might compete and need to leave ourselves open to conversations with other entrepreneurs about their products. If something we ask for is proprietary, then we ask entrepreneurs to provide what they can and we can dig deeper on an individual basis as needed.

Due diligence (DD) is often the part of the investment process that entrepreneurs hate. It can take much longer than they like, they are repeatedly peppered by investors with the same questions over and over, and after all the time and energy they spend on the process, there is often a "NO" at the end of the engagement. And secretly, most investors dislike the process as well. While we want to review all aspects of a potential investment and poke at the parts we do not feel are as sound or could use more detail, it is a tedious process for small funds such as ours, with limited staff and resources. Our general partners carried much of the DD load themselves and developed a streamlined process that worked well for us, but each group will have its own structure and procedures.

Once we decided to move a company into DD, one partner would volunteer to take the lead on reviewing the information gathered, following up with questions for the entrepreneur, and eventually producing a diligence report with their findings to share with the group. Another partner would co-lead and we engaged our fund associate to facilitate the information gathering and conduct additional outside research on market, competition, and general background information on the founder and the product or service. With Next Wave Impact Fund we led a similar process, with up to two DD leads from the investment committee as well as several of our limited partners volunteering to help with research and compiling the diligence report.

The diligence process can take a few weeks or a few months, depending on the readiness of the entrepreneur, the thoroughness of the documents provided, and the amount of time the investment group needs to review and ask further questions. The JumpFund worked hard to make our DD process less complicated and cumbersome, and also a more human process. We wanted to make it a two-way conversation and offer transparency and open communication about our expectations and interests. We wanted entrepreneurs to know it is ok to not have all the answers, but be prepared to address what you do know and not make up the rest. Honesty was always the best policy with our group, especially with our secret weapon Shelley, the psychologist, on our team. As Shelley liked to say, "I was listening for excuses... if they came back with rationalizations or dismissed what we were asking, that never sat well."

Since diligence is about de-risking an investment, I have seen companies derailed in their pursuit of funding at various stages of the DD process. If a red flag popped up in our review of a company's materials, a call with a client or other investor, or even an issue that arose during a basic background check, we would address these directly with the entrepreneur and if the answers were not to our satisfaction, we would back off from pursuing the deal. Some major red flags included—lack of full disclosure by an entrepreneur about something in their or the team's backgrounds; weak financials that did not chart a reasoned path to growth given key assumptions; a poor review by a client or partner; concerns from other investors who had dealt with the entrepreneur; or an entrepreneur not being able to produce the essential documents we had requested that would undergird their business model and path to exit.

Early on in our first fund's life cycle, we were very close to executing a certain deal and received some questionable information from a background report on a founder. Our background checks are relatively high level, with basic information on a person's finances and a search for any criminal activity—we use a local firm that works with corporate HR so the information we gather is similar to what would be sought when applying for any job. In this case, the founder had some personal financial management issues that were enough to make us suspect she might not be able to handle the finances of her own company.

Another time, we found out too late that a member of a company's team had a history of fraud and had been using an alias, then stole a large part of the company's technical code! Luckily, that investment was one of several smaller seed investments in a group of women-led companies out of an accelerator program so we didn't lose much. But these all point to why it is important for investors to do their homework and why trust and laying all one's cards on the table are a big part of entering into a relationship with a potential funder. If you're not willing to do that on the front end, it could come back to bite you in the future.

The reverse is also true for founders—*diligence potential investors*. Ask as many questions as you can before you go into pitch or even during DD as you also want to vet a potential investor. Call the CEOs of other companies in which they've invested, talk to founders you know who have been through their DD process, and certainly do extensive research on each of the partners to know your audience. Like any good job interview, a founder should come prepared with her queries to better understand what it will be like to work with a potential investor with whom she'll be sharing a piece of her company and even control if they take a board seat. In the end, this is all about relationships and trust which get even more complicated when money is involved. As an entrepreneur, go forth wisely and conduct your own diligence. You will thank yourself in the future for doing so.

Supporting Your Ecosystem

When we launched our second fund, we understood the need to hone our application process and provide an additional layer of information for female founders who were new to raising capital. Too many entrepreneurs were applying blindly for funding, with not even a basic understanding of what taking outside capital for their new company might mean or what constitutes an "investable" venture. Similar to other funds and networks, we began to offer monthly open office hours, to help new entrepreneurs ask questions prior to jumping into the pitch and diligence process. We developed a basic overview of both our thesis and angel investing as well as what an entrepreneur might need to check off before they approached us for capital. This overview is still available on our website today and one to which we often refer new entrepreneurs.

Due to the lack of access to capital, social networks, and general opportunity to learn about angel investing for first-time female founders when we launched our funds, it was important to us that we offered as much transparency and education as possible. Outside of our office hours, our partners often provided one-on-one coaching to those seeking funding, taking coffee meetings or calls to demystify the investment process and world of venture capital.

Hosting regular office hours eventually became unsustainable for our lean group of high-powered, busy women yet the gender lens investing ecosystem has evolved to offer many more resources for first-time entrepreneurs, which we can now direct those looking for funding. In the state of Tennessee, there are five local entrepreneur centers at which founders can find a wealth of information, connect with other entrepreneurs and investors, and get coaching and support. Many other states have similar support networks for entrepreneurs, some specifically directed toward women. There are also national support organizations such as NAWBO (National Association of Women Business Owners) or accelerator programs such as Springboard focused on female founders. During the pandemic, a wide variety of online resources, webinars, networking events, and panel discussions on everything from cap tables to creating strong pitch decks, became readily available. The Angel Capital Association launched several free webinars on "demystifying" angel investing and has new content specifically directed toward entrepreneurs.

Wherever you launch your fund or network, I highly recommend you engage with your local startup community and become available to coach or mentor new entrepreneurs. It is through these relationships that new social networks are formed and the mystery of angel investing is uncovered and made more accessible to first-time founders.

The Deal: A Marriage and Divorce

There have been entire books and workshops dedicated to learning the ins and outs of structuring the right deal both for the investor and the entrepreneur. In the end, both want a positive return on their investment in a successful startup. As a fund manager and active angel investor, I have seen many deal structures from SAFEs (simple agreement for equity) and convertible notes to aggressive preferred equity deals that are great for investors, but hard on founders. In its earliest days, JumpFund led only a few deals, so we were not always at the front end of decisions on key investment terms, but we did have some deal breakers. We also preferred equity or "priced" rounds over convertible notes or SAFES, which provided us as investors an additional layer of protection and leg up if an early exit were to take place.

What we found over time was that each deal is nuanced and we became more flexible on what we would accept as palatable if we felt strongly about the founder and company. Also, if we trusted or had a relationship with the "lead" investor (generally the one investing the most and setting the deal terms) we had a higher confidence that if they were in the deal we could get comfortable with whatever was negotiated. As mentioned before, a term sheet is similar to a prenuptial agreement, it guides who gets what both in the marriage and in the case of divorce. As an investor, you need to know what you are getting into and what will be the consequences, good or bad, if and when you get out of it. Setting the right terms or getting comfortable with those presented to you is one of the most important things you can do in establishing a strong founder-funder relationship from the outset.

As a newly established fund or angel investor, you should familiarize yourself with basic deal terms and structures so that you can effectively negotiate based on your group's risk tolerance and interests. Willing to take more risk and be more flexible and entrepreneur-friendly? Use a SAFE or Convertible Note, which are forms of debt, not equity, terms of which vary widely. These tend to be vehicles preferred by early stage entrepreneurs not yet ready to put a price or valuation on their company. Want to stick with a more traditional structure where investor rights, founder/CEO responsibilities, and ownership are more clearly defined? Invest in preferred equity, which generally means you have an investor "preference" and certain rights over the common (usually company founders) shareholders. And with an equity deal, the price per share or valuation of the company is clearly established by all owners.

Fundamental Angel Deal Structures

SAFE—Otherwise known as a Simple Agreement for Future Equity. If you are investing at a very early stage then the "price" or valuation of a company may have not yet been determined. The SAFE investment instrument was first developed by Y Combinator, one of the largest and longest running West Coast tech accelerators. These agreements allow you to transfer your investment into equity when there is a future-priced round of financing. SAFEs are often considered more "entrepreneur" friendly as they are not immediately giving up a piece of their company and do not necessarily have the interest or discounts often found in Convertible Notes.

Convertible Note—Just as they sound, these are "notes" or loan-like structures that convert when a priced round is consummated. Most angel investors will require that Convertible Notes include key terms such as a defined maturity date (at which the note would either convert or be paid back), interest (generally 5-8% for early stage companies), discounts (which means your dollars will go further in an equity round, commonly between 15-20% of the future priced share value) and/or a **valuation cap**, which keeps the future value of the company at a reasonable level to not dilute your potential ownership and also offers another way to calculate a "discount" if the difference between the company valuation in the next round is significantly higher than the cap.

Preferred Equity—Most angel investors prefer priced rounds in startup companies as it sets the valuation of the company and establishes ownership and investor rights. "Preferred" shares also trump common shares (held by founders and key employees). The percentage of preferred equity offered in an early stage company also can vary widely, but generally the "piece of the pie" offered to investors is in the 20-30% range, with some portion held back for future employees **(option pool)** and founder **vesting.** So, much like in Shark Tank lingo, if a company's **pre-money value** (value before investment) is priced at $5M and they are offering investors up to 20% ownership in the company, that means they are raising $1M in capital. If successful in their fundraising, the company would have a **post-money value** of $6M. A variety of easy cap table calculators are available online to simplify this math for both founders and investors.

As an investor or entrepreneur, I also encourage you to educate yourself on key deal terms available through angel investor education programs or online. Understanding the investment agreement you are signing can save you many headaches (and heartache) down the road. In the end, developing an understanding of basic terms and deal structures is important for any angel investor, but the bottom line is that you can come to a mutual agreement with the entrepreneur that feels beneficial to both sides. And it is always wise to check with legal counsel before signing any binding contract.

Deal terms, most often found in preferred equity rounds of financing, can vary widely, but several of those most important to JumpFund and many other angel investors include company valuation, investor and voting rights, participation rights, option pools, and future liquidity terms (see inset box for more detail on each of these). Make sure you know your rights, especially as the company grows and new investors potentially come in, creating additional layers of terms and conditions. For instance, a 2x liquidation preference for early investors may seem like a sweet deal, but down the line it may scare away other upstream investors and cram down the entrepreneur's final take so much that they may end up with nothing from the company they worked so hard to grow. Go in with eyes wide open and get comfortable with the basic language surrounding deal terms so that you don't get caught in an unfortunate, no-win situation when it comes time to exit the company.

Unfortunately, term sheets or a strong investor rights agreement cannot protect you if the company fails or is merged into another company for little to no value. Building a diverse portfolio will help mitigate the losses you will incur (and you will have them!) as will staying on top of the company's cap table with additional investment. As an early stage investor, you are banking on the few companies that make it big and whose return multiples are the sweetest for the earliest, most patient investors.

Basic Deal Terminology

Valuation—Company valuation establishes the price per share and the ownership structure in an equity round of financing. Think of this as the company's price tag, often referred to as the "pre-money" valuation. Valuations for early stage companies differ widely from region to region (NY and Silicon Valley based companies generally garner higher valuations) and across industries (tech versus consumer goods, etc) or competitive markets. Early stage investors may use several methods to help determine valuation, especially when a company has little to no revenue on which to base a predictive company value. The **Berkus** or **Scorecard** methods are helpful when a company may not yet have real revenue but instead can be "scored" on qualitative values such as Team, Business Model, Intellectual Property, or Minimum Viable Product (MVP). Ideally, company valuation (and thus the unrealized value of your investment) grows with each new funding round in which a new, and hopefully increased, value is established based on growth trends, revenues, and/or other metrics on which the company and market places inherent value (patents, user base, etc).

Investor Rights—Access to financial and company information to which shareholders are privy. These rights sometimes depend on the size of the check you write as larger investors often have preference over others. Yet, it is wise for early stage companies to keep their investors abreast of all aspects of the company, good, bad, or ugly. Investors are more likely to stick with you for the long haul if they feel there has been strong communication and transparency.

Voting Rights—Some early investors ask for a board of directors seat or at least a seat for their "class" or round in which they invested (eg. a Series A shareholder representative). Shareholder voting power is also critical as these companies grow and make key decisions. Some company decisions, especially those that impact fundraising or future valuation which have a direct impact on investors, will be put to an all-shareholder vote based on percentage interest in the company. Some agreements also include "drag along" rights that allow a company to make key decisions with only a majority of the shareholders (aka those holding the biggest piece of the pie).

Participation Rights or ROFR (right of first refusal)—As companies grow, they will likely raise more capital, and (ideally) each round will increase in value and thus price. Most early stage investors plan to hold back some portion of their capital for "follow-on" rounds so that they can continue to hold onto their percentage of equity for as long as possible or at least not become too fully diluted. As an investor, it is important then to include a ROFR and/or Participation rights clause in your agreements to at least have the option to participate in subsequent rounds of financing.

Option Pool—Some portion (10-15%) of the company's ownership is generally preserved for future hires and company growth, important for early stage companies that often pay or hire their employees with equity bonuses, a promise of what is to come. It is standard for new option pools to be set aside in each subsequent round of investment to offer additional value to existing key employees as well as help recruit new talent as the company grows.

Liquidity—Maybe the most important part of a term sheet, the liquidity clause will detail how investors plan to make a return on their investment. Most are fairly standard, offering liquidity only if a company is acquired or, more rarely for angel investors, IPOs (initial public offering). In some cases, early investors may ask for a higher than 1x liquidity or include certain terms for buying back shares or a guaranteed return if the company does not have a clear path to a positive exit.

The rule of thumb when companies take outside capital is "last in, first out" with any debt being on top of the heap. Whatever funds are left in the company or come from a transaction will go to those investors/debtors who most recently put in their money, not the earliest investors. This always seems somewhat unfair as those who fronted the company in its early days took the most risk, and those later on had likely better metrics and more data to assess whether it would be a good investment. Yet, if the company does exceedingly well, the earliest investors will have the highest return multiples. If you do have the ability to continue to "follow on" with your investment, you will have the most advantage, staying relevant on the cap table and taking advantage of being first in AND first out. Although make sure it is still a company you feel strongly will produce outsized returns—it's better to walk away than pour more money into a sinking company and never get any of it back.

The JumpFund certainly has experienced both wins and losses across both portfolios. As I write this, we are currently heading toward the tail end of the life span of our first fund, which was ten years with two one-year extensions. Our second fund is right in the middle of the common "life cycle" of an angel investment fund—fully invested but still a ways to go with portfolio management. Both funds have so far weathered the storms of early company failures and are poised to reap strong returns with our remaining companies. Our second fund has experienced stronger IRR (internal rate of return) growth as we were able to reinvest or "follow on" in several of our strongest performers from our first fund. We also have grown and matured as a group of early stage investors and nurtured relationships with other gender lens funds and networks to help source the highest prospects.

Early stage investment funds generally follow a "J" curve gain/loss profile. During the fund's investment period, money is going out the door and is most likely fully deployed within a five-year period. This is also a very vulnerable, volatile time for a fund's portfolio companies, and there will likely be more losses than gains while companies are proving their business models and may sink or swim.

After the investment period, as companies are maturing and gaining more traction and value, the internal rate of return should begin to tick up, although there may still be attrition of companies in the portfolio. Higher gains tend to come later in the portfolio's life span, during the "harvest" period, where companies are beginning to exit and those with the highest value maturation will ideally make up for those who are laggards or "wind down" altogether.

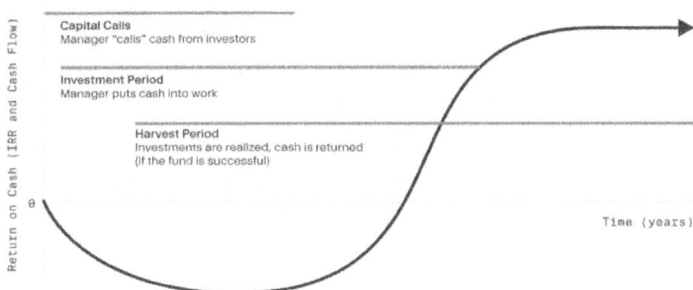

Several of our early investments folded due to internal company failures—mismanagement, not getting to market fast enough, dwindling cash resources, or misjudging their product/market fit. While others were the victims of outside forces such as bad deals with investors, market volatility (pandemic!), or new, competing technologies. While you help as many companies in your portfolio as you can for as long as possible, sometimes they are just not salvageable. Still others have saved face with investors by merging with other companies with similar services, often without monetary compensation but a transfer of ownership so that the investors still have a piece of some pie, albeit a much smaller percentage. There are many ways a company might "wind down," so be prepared to weather all of the ups and downs with the promise of a few bright stars who will refill your coffers and help them overflow with returns to your investors.

One company success story I have been involved with on my angel investor journey is Nepris, led by founder/CEO Sabari Raja. Nepris was the very first investment of Next Wave Impact Fund and I served as the deal lead. A STEM education platform, Nepris connected industry professionals directly into K-12 classrooms to help grow students' content and career knowledge in science, technology, engineering and math as well as a variety of other subjects. At its height, Nepris serviced hundreds of school districts across the country and tens of thousands of students and teachers. Sabari was a gracious, extremely driven founder with a heart for her company's mission to help students gain a greater perspective on what is possible for them in the STEM fields and ignite more curiosity and interest in hard to teach subject areas such as organic chemistry, industrial engineering, or computational biology.

Next Wave was among the first "Seed" stage investors in Nepris in 2017 and invested again in their Series A round a few years later. In December 2021, the company was acquired by a private equity firm specializing in EdTech and workforce development. Our patient capital and subsequent follow-on investment reaped a 3x return overall, but an 8x return on our initial $100k investment. It was our first big "win" for the Next Wave Impact Fund and I am proud to have been the company's liaison, keeping in close communication with the founder and helping her with connections and resources along the way. This is an example of a strong portfolio return and why being able to keep back some "dry powder" to continue to invest when the going is good can pay off.

Stand by Your Woman

When SuperFanU, the first portfolio company we invested in with our first fund sold to PrestoSports in 2021, I sent bourbon and flowers to the co-founder and CEO Kayla Mount (which as a good Kentuckian she preferred to champagne). I had worked with Kayla and former CEO Tendai Charasika to grow SuperFanU since 2014, and I served on the board representing the Seed stage investors. The sale of the company produced modest returns to investors as well as the prospect of an additional "earnout" for the founders if sales increased over the next 18 months. Upon receiving the gift Kayla texted me:

> *"I truly appreciate everything you and JumpFund have done for me over the years. The JumpFund was more than a check. Not only you, but the other partners were always accessible. You have been a sounding board and mentor. I am so grateful. Now I am going to kick this earnout's ass."*

At JumpFund, our intent is to "add value beyond the check." As a smaller sized fund with limited dollars to invest in any one company, we are looking to build relationships with founders that support them in other ways, not just monetarily. We have served as active board members or observers in several of our companies. Each of our general partners has several companies to which they are assigned as direct liaisons and keep tabs on company updates, meet with founders on a regular basis, and direct any company needs to our partners or larger capital network. With the help of our 100+ limited partners, we have supported our portfolio companies to define HR strategies and establish diversity focused hiring practices; streamlined manufacturing and reduced product costs; addressed IP and legal issues; reviewed marketing plans and SEO strategies, and coached myriad founders through the ups and downs of the startup grind.

One particular example is our long-term involvement with Emily Morris, founder/CEO of our portfolio company, EMRGY, a modular hydropower manufacturer based in Atlanta. Kim Seals, our Atlanta partner has worked most directly with Emily over the years, coaching her on everything from pitch prep to client pipeline development and human resource management. Our wide network has also provided EMRGY support, including Kim's brother-in-law, an engineer who saw the company's potential early on and helped her connect to the right resources to launch her first full scale product pilot with the Bureau of Land Management in Colorado. We also connected Emily with a JumpFund limited partner who has a deep background in mechanical engineering and manufacturing. He introduced her to Tennessee-based parts manufacturers who were able to significantly reduce her cost of goods and ultimately increase her profit margins on the turbines by 30%.

As Kim says, "It is these personal connections and the deep ownership we take in mentoring, coaching and developing these entrepreneurs that make a difference." Such connections are certainly not unheard of in the angel investing space, where investors often become deeply involved in the companies in which they invest. But it has certainly not been the case for most female founders, who do not usually have the same network of support or cheerleaders to help them grow their companies.

We are also supportive of our mompreneurs, as almost half of our company founders have become mothers (or had second and third children) while successfully running their companies. Our woman-led fund understands the challenges of running a successful business alongside motherhood. In fact, Tiffanie, one of our own partners, had all three of her boys in the process of launching and running our fund as well as her own startup AND sitting on our local school board! And while *we* celebrate these badass founder mamas as strong, resilient women who can multi-task and juggle all of the things it takes to succeed, women often do not divulge to other potential investors that they are pregnant or even have children, as that is usually seen as a marker against them. Female founders who are mothers are always asked how they have time to "do it all." We know from experience that while we may not always be able to do it all, we certainly can do many things well at the same time, including running a business.

Having built a portfolio of over thirty companies, across both JumpFund I and JumpFund II, the work of keeping up with a wide array of founders across industries is sometimes daunting. While we keep tabs on a quarterly basis with all of our companies, requesting company updates and financials at least four times a year, we have found ways to establish deeper, trusted relationships with many of our founders, offering an open door for advice, coaching, or at times, a literal shoulder to cry on. Entrepreneurship is hard, and being a female founder is 10x harder. All of our founders let us know that they appreciate our perspective and support as women in business and work to maintain open lines of communication and transparency with us as we do with them.

Celebrating Success

In the early stage, angel investing game, it is widely known that you win some and lose some. In fact, when we pitched our funds to potential investors, we always led with the risk inherent in this type of investment and that our ultimate goal was to choose at least a few top companies that may likely carry the returns of the entire portfolio. Out of the more than 30 companies invested in by both funds, 16 currently remain active. Those "left standing" have been significantly increasing in value, with additional funding rounds, revenue growth, and client traction and we anticipate that most, if not all, will find a profitable exit. A few of our portfolio companies are currently valued at over $100M and one shining star over $200M. And since we invested early, when their valuations were $5-10M we will likely see a very profitable return on our investments (ROI).

While there have been a few "wins," several of our portfolio losses have been especially painful as we were close to the entrepreneurs and knew we had done all we could to help them succeed. Some company failures were due to market fit, lack of adequate traction to sustain growth, or team dynamics that worked against forward progress. Others were dealt a fatal blow, such as the company that did not time its organic certification renewal with new orders and thus had to pull all of its existing stock from big supermarket accounts. Or when a supply chain partner literally stopped producing the goods due to demand from larger clients, holding the company materials hostage in the process. Or the company that found out its outsourced CTO was masquerading under a pseudonym and was wanted for fraud in another state!

Yet, we were cautioned from the beginning to take these losses in stride and focus on those companies that are able to go the distance and take us, and them, over the finish line. Our first fund has already realized two successful exits, one early on and one more recently. The first was a quick ride with a stellar entrepreneur who has gone on to do other great things and pay it forward for other undervalued entrepreneurs. The second exit came after years of intensive work with the company management team through our position on their board of directors. Neither were 10X multiple exits (the golden chalice of angel investing) but were positive exits for the companies in their own rights.

JumpFund's first, successful exit was a highly touted success for a Black, woman-led company in the Southeast. Partpic was founded by Jewel Burks Solomon in 2013 and JumpFund was introduced to the company by William Crowder, then lead partner of Catalyst Ventures, an offshoot of Comcast Ventures, which targeted funding towards diverse founders. We had also followed Jewel and her award winning pitches at several regional startup events including 3686, Rise of the Rest, SXSW and TechCrunch Disrupt. And in 2015, Jewel pitched Partpic to President Obama at the first entrepreneurial Demo Day to be held in the White House.

Jewel had leveraged her experience working in the industrial parts industry, literally sourcing mechanical parts for clients using a paper bound catalog, into developing Partpic's platform for digital parts visualization and identification. The idea was revolutionary in this antiquated industry, and immediately garnered interest from Home Depot and Delta, interested in helping customers search more effectively for the right screw or bolt or their mechanical repair teams locate the right parts on a more efficient basis. In practice, a client would snap a photo of the part they wish to identify on their phone and Partpic's algorithms would determine the manufacturer, model number and size to order a replacement.

In addition to Jewel as CEO, the company had built a diverse, rockstar team of engineers and operators. Jason Crain, co-founder and COO, helped Partpic land several early corporate pilots for the company to test the technology as well as $2M in startup capital. The computer vision technology for Partpic was designed and built by Dr. Nashalie Sephus, an engineer who went on to serve as Amazon's Applied Science Manager for their AI team. The JumpFund was particularly drawn to the diversity, depth, and breadth of the team, as well as 24-year-old Burks Solomon's engaging persona and clear fit as CEO.

Fast forward two years, and Partpic received an offer they couldn't refuse from Amazon, who was interested in integrating the part-finder technology into their own search platform. Although this acquisition took place at an early stage for the company, and Jewel will tell you that was not her original plan, it did give the team the opportunity to continue to develop their product in Atlanta as part of Amazon's Visual Search and AR (augmented reality) team. In 2018, Amazon released *Partfinder* in its mobile shopping app.

Raising capital was not easy as a Black woman in the Southeast, and Jewel hit many of the biases and roadblocks faced by women and BIPOC founders. When she went out for next round funding to expand the company, before the offer from Amazon, she faced an uphill battle convincing VCs that Partpic's technology was worth investment. In the end, it was their loss and her (and our) gain.

Our early investment in Partpic and Jewel paid off beyond a simple return of capital. We were proud to have supported a young, Black, female founder as she was just launching toward her future success and even more ecstatic that she has paid her early success forward and continues to help other underrepresented entrepreneurs. In a conversation with Jewel early on in our funder-founder relationship, she intimated that someday she hoped to have a fund of her own that could help elevate more entrepreneurs like her. Today, Jewel has become Head of Google for Startups, increasing access for BIPOC and female founders, and co-founded her own venture fund, Collab Capital, aimed at closing the gap in funding for Black founders.

Another win for both JumpFund I and II was the sale of SuperFan to PrestoSports. This was a much longer journey, and began with SuperFan as our very first investment by JumpFund I back in 2014. We were drawn to this team for its leadership diversity—female co-founder/COO with a white male CTO/co-founder, and a Black male CEO—as well as the industry, sports fan engagement. SuperFan had developed a white-labeled mobile app for college, university and high school sports teams to engage directly with their fan base and already had many logos on their roster.

One reason we were drawn to the company was that as a former Assistant Dean, part of my role was to place ads for student recruitment as well as alumni development. A clear path to many eyeballs was through the athletic department, and in particular college football, a huge pastime in the South with dedicated fans and business sponsorship. But instead of a one-time game day marquee or insert in a program, what if our business school ads were beamed into every fan's mobile phone as they checked the scores or bought their tickets?

Thus, our interest in this intriguing company from Louisville, KY grew and eventually, we placed our first bet on them. Our initial $100,000 investment in SuperFan expanded to an additional $150K alongside other Kentucky-based investors. While we worked to get larger VCs interested, the company continued to grow its customer base and services and became one of the leaders in the mobile, sports fan space. Eight years later, our original bet paid off, and another sports tech company, Presto Sports, which specializes in website versus mobile interfaces, saw great value in adding SuperFan to its offerings.[27]

This was also a company we leaned into heavily beyond the check. From the time of our initial investment, I joined the Board of Directors and later became Chair as we navigated the company's exit. I worked closely with co-founders Kayla and Chris and former CEO Tendai to determine company strategy and was always looking out for potential partnerships or investors. In early 2020, the company made the difficult decision to right-size its team and move out of their spacious startup offices to work completely remotely and preserve cash. This proved to be a prescient move as within three months the pandemic set in, putting a halt to almost all college and high school sports and the company had to rely on the Payroll Protection Plan (PPP) loans to make it through.

Later that year, Kayla took over as CEO, steering the company through lean times, yet eventually coming out on top through the sale to Presto at an opportune time. With an earnout structure and diligence on the part of Bluegrass Angels, a lead investor in the company, Jump-Fund ultimately realized almost 2X on its overall investment. And, the SuperFan founding team was able to realize the continued utilization of its fan engagement platform within another sports fan engagement company. The ending of this funder-founder story is ultimately about perseverance and grit ending in a win-win deal for all parties involved.

Growing Minicorns

Celebrating our portfolio's wins, whether they are 2X or 10X, is incredibly important to our mission. Our ultimate goal is to prove that female entrepreneurs are worthy of investment and that women-led venture firms investing with a gender lens do not compromise strong returns. Attracting more women into angel investing was the first step, building women's leadership in venture capital was the second, and making savvy, lucrative investments in women-led ventures is the ultimate proof that our model works. As general partners managing JumpFund's investments we are working for the "carry" or that additional 20% split we will obtain only if our returns are above the initial investment of our investors' capital. Every positive return gets us closer to that goal and proves that women-led companies are just as investable as those led by men.

When we started JumpFund, there were few examples of women-led startups that had become "unicorns" or hit the $1B valuation mark which is a rare occurrence for any startup. I even had a hard time coming up with a list of female founders who had recognizable companies that were over $5M in assets. Fast forward ten years and there are more women leading companies who are killing valuation metrics and making strong returns for their investors. Three women-led companies went public (IPO) in 2021—Bumble (dating app), FIGS (health apparel), and 23andMe (genetic tests). And many more joined the Unicorn Club, some more household names than others, including Maven Clinic (women's digital health services) and BlockFi (crypto currency lending). Several have also become "decacorns" valued at over $10B such as Talkdesk (cloud based contact center) or Nubank (Brazilian digital bank).[28] Yet, the unicorn club remains male dominated, a statistic JumpFund and others are working hard to change. According to Crunchbase (2021), "the unicorn club has always been open to men and women, but in the five-plus years tracking venture-backed companies valued at $1 billion and up, the vast majority have had all-male founding teams."

The JumpFund is proud to have a few companies rising in valuation ranks and being recognized as "minicorns." Tracxn, a platform providing market intelligence and tracking of startups and private markets, categorizes "minicorns" as "early startups with good potential to grow due to either big market size or great execution in a small market." Savvy, early stage angel investors understand that most if not all startups we fund will realistically exit in the millions, not billions in company value. And although we'd love to lasso a unicorn, our lane is generally investing in and nurturing companies to successful exits through acquisition, not IPO.

One of JumpFund's investments that could be considered a minicorn is Bark, an app and platform dedicated to helping parents and schools monitor and protect kids on social media. Bark is currently valued at over $200M, having closed a Series C (later stage) fundraise of $90M in early 2022. Bark is run by a diverse team led by CPO (chief parent officer) Titania Jordan and CEO Brian Bason. In 2023, Bark analyzed more than 5.6 billion messages across texts, email, YouTube, and 30+ apps and social media platforms generated on devices used by over 7 million children. Their software identified potentially threatening instances of violence, sexual predators, drugs, mental health, and cyberbullying amongst tweens and teens and helped parents and schools identify those most at risk. Bark is rapidly growing its partnerships with companies such as CenturyLink, Microsoft, and Lenovo to expand its reach and company value, including launching the Bark Phone in 2022. We anticipate Bark will be one of several JumpFund portfolio companies to garner exceptional returns and as moms of kids using social media, Bark is a company we are proud to have been a part of growing to make the world a better place.

Several other companies in our portfolio are making significant strides, including: EMRGY, a modular hydropower company; Motivo, a virtual clinical supervision platform for mental health professionals; and Funding U, a non co-sign student loan resource for last gap lending. All of these companies have recently closed Series A or B rounds of financing and are valued at over $20M. Well on their way to becoming the next women-led minicorns.

Women Supporting Women:
EMRGY & JumpFund

At age 24, Emily Morris was a young, female founder on a mission. Straight out of Georgia Tech in Atlanta, she and her father had developed a proprietary new magnetic turbine technology for modular, small-scale (about the size of a small school bus) hydropower production. She had grand visions of disrupting the cleantech market, which was primarily focused on wind and solar energy by reinventing hydropower to be used in "slow flow" waterways, such as municipal canals where EPA regulations on fish and wildlife would not be an impediment. With only a pilot model and a robust business plan for expansion across the U.S. and globally, Emily began to pitch angel investors for seed capital to underwrite the production and deployment of her first hydropower units.

Her experience as a young woman in this male-dominated industry was difficult and riddled with bias and injustices from the very beginning. Early on, she remembers repeatedly pitching to all-male groups in the Southeast and being met with condescension and outright bias, with the investors preferring to direct questions about the technology, market, and her financial model to her newly-minted male COO instead of to her as CEO and the one pitching the company. When it came to negotiating her first term sheet, she felt taken advantage of and bullied by the lead investor, who redlined their initial agreement and significantly reduced her control and power in the company. Luckily, that investor ended up walking away from the deal while others in his group came in to fully fund their portion. "That experience made me realize that investors were going to see me as a target that they could take advantage of," says Emily "which led me to a desire to work with empathetic investors, people who know what it's like to walk in a woman's shoes."

We met Emily in 2014, when she had first approached Golden Seeds for funding, but had only her initial patents and no customers with whom to pilot her first hydropower units. Fast forward a year, and she had won a \$1M Department of Energy grant and was off to the races. EMRGY had also successfully secured its first pilot with Southern Companies, a regional utility company, and JumpFund was impressed with her progress. We were interested in diversifying our portfolio with clean technology and saw great potential in Emily as a founder. In 2016, we placed our bet alongside her first seed investors and began what has become a deep and mutually beneficial relationship with Emily and the success of EMRGY.

According to Emily, JumpFund's investment has always been much more than a check. She sees her relationship with us as more "approachable and accessible" than many of her other investors and considers both our general partners and several of our limited partners, who have brought deep expertise and guidance, as her ad hoc "advisory board." The JumpFund has offered her coaching and mentoring around talent, organizational structure and growth strategy leadership, HR compliance, and even manufacturing. Through our partner network we have also been able to connect Emily with regional resources to produce her hydropower units at a much lower cost and land her first full deployment of a 10 unit hydroelectric "array" in collaboration with Denver Water and the Bureau of Land Management As our general partner based in Atlanta, Kim Seals has stayed close to Emily, mentoring her through human resource and strategic growth challenges, including helping her recently hire a female CFO.

While JumpFund is not as deeply engaged with all of our companies, we have developed a special connection with Emily and have appreciated her willingness to reach out in times of need, use us as a sounding board, and build a trusted and mutually beneficial relationship. When her company was in a difficult place with a large, early investor pressuring her to repay in full a note that the company could not afford and would push them into bankruptcy, JumpFund stepped in. We helped rally a few "friendly" investors to help her with a short-term loan with favorable terms to get her through the crisis and continue to grow the company and position her successfully to attract next-stage investors. She has since completed an $18M Series B raise with new, strategic investors with cleantech portfolios. Over the years, she has felt that we are a group of women she can turn to with difficult questions and receive honest and constructive feedback, helping drive the destiny of her company.

"Through JumpFund you have access to such a broad range of experience, talent, and skill sets. And at the end of the day, the most important thing is the eagerness and willingness to jump in. I think one of the things that is so hard for an entrepreneur is the vast number of people who say, 'feel free to bounce something off of me.' We (entrepreneurs) don't want a wall that we can bounce something off of, we want someone that's actually engaging and notices what is happening in your business. When I'm around JumpFund (you) ask the hard questions and are open to and completely non-judgmental of the answers, digging in and driving the destiny that you want to see in the fund. For instance, you wanted to see me drive 30% of cost out of my product, and you have someone in your group that helped me do that. It's a win-win when the company becomes better, and drives value back to the investors."

—Emily Morris, CEO/founder EMRGY

ACT V

The Rise of Women Angel Leaders

5

The Rise of Women Angel Leaders

Funding is the new feminism — we need more women investors at all stages seed, VC, private equity, especially as women are the fastest growing segment of entrepreneurs globally.

—Heather Henyon, Mindshift Capital

Building it for Ourselves

It has only been a short time, over the past fifteen or so years, that women have been actively engaged in investing in early stage ventures and discovered the power and influence of this asset class. Vanguards such as Golden Seeds have led the way to educate more women about angel investing and create structure and support for those wanting to dip their toe in these foreign waters. Since we launched JumpFund in 2013, we have been part of a rising tide of women banding together and growing the impact of our capital in the startup ecosystem. Within a short period, a significant number of women-led angel funds and networks, as well as larger venture firms such as Cowboy Ventures and Female Founders Fund, have arisen and influenced this landscape.

As I've mentioned previously, when we launched our first fund we quickly realized how few women were angel investors and even fewer were leading angel networks or serving as fund managers. With the number of women as active angel investors growing to upwards of 35% of all angels (from only 5% in 2013), we were part of a "rising tide" of women who came to angel investing in large part due to the inequalities facing female founders in the entrepreneurial marketplace. These women are reshaping the conversation in angel investing not only to open doors for other women and more diverse founders, but also to consider a wider lens of companies with social and environmental impact at their core or solving for problems specifically faced by women.

Over the past ten years of engaging with the Angel Capital Association I have witnessed this rising tide first hand and seen how women have influenced the conversation around angel investing. We now have whole segments of our annual ACA conference devoted to impact investing, investors and founders of color, the importance of DEI (diversity, equity, and inclusion) in our work, and see a strong representation of female founders in our annual innovation showcase. Our presence and influence has changed the dynamics of angel investing, I believe for the good, and many of our male colleagues feel the same. Even our ACA board of directors now has close to fifty percent female representation. And we have a robust and active group of angel investors (women and men) engaged in our Growing Women's Capital syndication network where we share women-led company deals and nurture more women as angels and group leaders.

The following are profiles of several female fund managers in our women's capital ecosystem, each addressing the dearth of women as angel investors as well as expanding greater access to funding for women-led ventures across the U.S. and globally. It is with these funds, networks, and female partners that JumpFund has found its greatest allies and connections that helped our two small funds in the Southeast U.S. to have even greater success and impact. I am grateful for these bold, savvy, badass women who have been my mentors and co-conspirators in this work and taught me much along the way. I hope they will inspire you to think boldly and follow your own path to invest in the change you want to see in the world.

Alicia Robb: Rising Tide and Next Wave Impact

In 2016, I first connected with Alicia Robb, angel investor, fund manager, author, and researcher on entrepreneurial finance. I learned about her initial efforts to launch her first angel fund to engage women investors at a social gathering of women at an Angel Capital Association conference in San Diego, a few years after we'd launched Jump-Fund. At this conference, these women were excitedly talking about a new fund they had joined, called the Rising Tide. The premise of the fund stemmed from research Alicia and co-author Susan Coleman had conducted on financing strategies for women-owned firms in their first book, *A Rising Tide*. The first Rising Tide fund was composed of 100 women each committing $10,000 to pool their capital and launch a $1M fund dedicated to investing in women-led ventures. The idea was that by introducing women to this asset class of angel investing at a much lower level than traditional venture funds (many start at a minimum $250,000 commitment) and providing them with a network of other women learning the ropes together, we could begin to get women off the sidelines and engage more women's capital in early stage investing to start changing the narrative for female entrepreneurs.

Rising Tide was such a hit in the U.S. that Alicia went on to support the creation of Rising Tide Europe and Rising Tide Africa due to interest from the global entrepreneurship and angel investing workshops she led. Two of Rising Tide's early investments, OtoSense (an at-home ear infection detector) and UnaliWear (smart watch for elderly), have had great success and proven the impact of this small but mighty fund. The premise was similar to JumpFund's first fund—create an entry point that is more accessible to women who are starting out on their early stage investing journey and provide them an education and support network along the way. The goal was to activate women's capital so they might see its potential and impact and go on to explore other opportunities in this asset class.

Alicia came to angel investing through her work in global microfinance as well as research on small business financing for the SBA (Small Business Administration) and Federal Reserve. She then spent 12 years working at the Kauffman Foundation conducting research on the gender and racial gaps in high growth entrepreneurship. When she looked into reasons behind these gaps, she discovered that very few early stage investors were women or people of color and she wanted to understand why. She found that women and investors of color had not been exposed to this asset class and knew very little about it and had also not seen companies with which they had an affinity to invest in. Her first Rising Tide fund was launched while she was still at Kauffman with the premise that by engaging and educating a more diverse investor base, more funding would be directed towards companies led by women and founders of color.

Alicia's Rising Tide experiment gave way to a larger, second fund called Next Wave Impact Fund. Many of the same investors from Rising Tide joined Next Wave and Alicia circled an experienced group of women angels, some of whom had been limited partners in the first fund, to serve on its investment committee (IC). Alicia was interested in engaging women leaders in the IC from across the country, representing different geographies and viewpoints, all with some angel investing or fund experience themselves. It was at this point that she was referred to me, who had watched Rising Tide from afar and admired what they had built but at the time was laser focused on building our second fund. I was intrigued to join a group of women with angel investing leadership roles similar to mine.

Taking a seat on the IC for Next Wave Impact Fund was

a game changer for me even as a seasoned fund manager. Launched in 2017, we conducted all of our formation, limited partner, and pitch meetings via Zoom (yes, pre-pandemic!) as our partners were spread across the country and we wanted easy, equitable access for entrepreneurs. Next Wave provided education and support for its limited partners with its progressive "learning by doing" fund model. It harnessed the knowledge that women participating in this asset class were hungry for education and mentoring which would ultimately make them more successful and savvy angel investors. All limited partners were invited (virtually) to each monthly pitch meeting where an IC member would take the lead on Q&A with the entrepreneur, followed by a closed session during which the LPs could listen in on the IC discussion of whether or not to move the company forward into due diligence.

Once a path for the company was determined by the IC, Next Wave LPs were invited to join a diligence committee led by one of the IC members so as to learn that process and roll up their sleeves on whatever topic they were more interested or experienced in, whether that be finance, HR, sales or marketing. The final investment decision was made by the IC, but the LPs had a voice all along the way and had the chance to add value and perspective to the decision-making process.

Next Wave also had a slightly different thesis than JumpFund, with a focus on "impact driven" companies using the United Nations' SDGs (social & developmental goals) as its guiding star. This new lens helped me to personally diversify my early stage investing portfolio as well as consider JumpFund investments through an impact lens. My involvement with Next Wave also allowed me to work with women around the world, from Dubai and Paris to the Bay Area, to develop a portfolio of 15 companies, diversified across industry and geography, all of which were led by women and/or people of color. The Next Wave IC members, a group of nine phenomenal women, have become my core group of advisors as I've continued to grow as an angel investor and leader in this space.

As Next Wave states on its website, "Together, we are creating the next wave of educated and trained angel investors focused on both social impact and financial returns and are investing in underrepresented entrepreneurs." For those building a fund or network by women for women, Next Wave is a unique model of how to incorporate angel investor education and training into your fund management and portfolio development process. And it is a prime example of women angels "doing it for ourselves," creating the platforms and supportive network environments that showcase how women want to engage in this asset class.

Sara Brand & Kerry Rupp: True Wealth Ventures

Since being introduced to venture capital in the Bay Area early in her career, Sara has felt her life's purpose was to be a VC. Starting in mechanical engineering with three degrees from the University of Texas and UC Berkeley, she was one of only a handful of women in leadership positions in the semiconductor industry. Yet, she did not understand the lack of women in her industry until she was asked to represent her company at a global women's forum and realized there were very few women at her level doing comparable work on the technical, engineering side of the business.

Having worked earlier in her career as an analyst at McKenzie, she dug into the data and discovered a 2017 report on "Gender Matters" which highlighted both the lack of women in technology as well as their outperformance in senior leadership.[29] From her earlier days in venture capital, she realized that there was an untapped business opportunity at hand, especially, as the report indicated, businesses with more women in senior management were outperforming those with all-male teams. The McKinsey data on publicly traded, women-led companies showed that those with women in senior leadership positions saw significantly higher financial performance. "I realized it was the best investment and business opportunity I had ever seen," recalls Sara.

Sara also began to put the puzzle pieces together around women's leadership and the potential social and environmental impact of companies. In her experience, she had seen many women starting companies that were making a positive impact. "On the University of Texas College of Engineering advisory board we're always trying to attract and retain more women engineers," says Sara, "and they are almost universally focused on improving environmental or human health when they come into engineering." Sara also realized there were no venture funds in Texas focused on the confluence of women and impact, although lots of entrepreneurship.

Yet Sara was very comfortable and satisfied with her current position on the senior leadership team at Advanced Micro Devices, a leader in semiconductor engineering, and did not see a path forward to pursue her dream of starting her own venture firm. In fact, time and again Sara would create a spreadsheet, as any good operations manager would do, that outlined the pros and cons of jumping into venture capital or staying in her very respectable, breadwinning job. Each time, the pros of staying in her job would loudly outweigh the cons so she powered on. It was not until she got physically, terribly sick during an extended family vacation that she realized her body might be telling her something even though making the decision to leave corporate America was not at all "rational."

Enter Kerry Rupp. Sara met Kerry in December, 2014

and their first lunch meeting, which ended up lasting several hours, quickly turned into a partnership and they started fundraising for True Wealth less than a year later. Sara had finally found the one other woman in venture capital in the state of Texas at that time and she knew she'd found the right partner to help launch a fund. Kerry had joined DreamIt Ventures, a top ten U.S. startup accelerator and fund as CEO in 2010. During her tenure, Dreamit launched a $20M follow-on investment fund for its accelerator companies as well as two programs focused on underrepresented founders—DreamIt Access for BIPOC entrepreneurs and DreamIt Athena for female entrepreneurs.

Unlike Sara, Kerry was not sure she wanted to commit the rest of her career to venture capital, as she had seen the "dark side" of VCs and preferred her work at DreamIt nurturing and launching entrepreneurs. Yet what intrigued her was this huge white space and lack of access to capital for women entrepreneurs, which she had witnessed helping launch DreamIt Athena. She was compelled by the idea that launching a woman-led VC firm was really its own startup with a problem to solve and new product to sell.

"I remember that the data was out there about the 2% of funding going to women," says Kerry. At Dreamit she had worked with the Chamber of Commerce and other entities to look at the Austin, TX entrepreneurial ecosystem data to see if it was similar to the national data for female founders. She found that the same 2% statistic of dollars invested in women was also true in her own backyard.

Together, Sara and Kerry make the consummate team. Sara loves the process and operations side of running a firm while Kerry is an entrepreneur at heart and enjoys the "sales" side of fundraising and pitching. Like Jump-Fund, they saw a problem on both sides of the market and the potential power of harnessing women as investors to change fundamental gender dynamics. True Wealth successfully raised $19M for their first fund, of which eighty percent were female investors.

Sara and Kerry also knew from their extensive research that women make eighty percent of all consumer decisions, especially in the arena of health and wellness. As Sara points out, "Women are seeing problems that are critical to environmental and human health and have unique insights in terms of solutions." Thus, their first True Wealth fund focused primarily on women-led startups building consumer-facing products and services which improved human or environmental health. Their sweet spot were early stage companies in which they could be the lead investor and serve on the board of directors, helping to guide the company with their extensive operations and business backgrounds.

Fundraising as first-time, female fund managers in the state of Texas was not easy. Initially, they focused on women outside their own networks, speaking at women's groups and trying to build momentum with like-minded investors who understood their thesis and fund's imperative. Kerry remembers that she specifically did not target women in her immediate friend groups, including her Harvard Business School network, as she felt there was a cultural bias to not talk about investments as women. When they surveyed their limited partners after one of their semi-annual fund dinners, they found that the majority were all new to venture capital and had never been asked or invited to join any other funds.

For their second fundraise, Kerry wrote what she calls a "manifesto" to her friends outlining True Wealth's mission and vision and making sure that all the women in her network felt invited and encouraged to join their movement. Kerry shared her missive to women in her network, which led with: "Hey, absolutely no obligation for you to invest with us, if it's not a fit, but we should be telling each other about these things. You should have an invitation and feel like you're educated on what you need to know, to make a decision as opposed to it being hidden and not shared."

Ultimately, Kerry and Sara's BHAG (big hairy audacious goal) would be the imperative for funds with a gender focus to go away. With Pitchbook still reporting less than 2% of venture capital going to female founders, they see this as a very long way off. Originally, they were going to subtitle their first fund "Gender Matters" after the McKenzie report data on the outperformance of companies with women at the helm, because they felt with their fund and the increase in other women-led funds nationwide, they could quickly address this gender gap in access to capital and move on to other underrepresented founders. After nine years of doing this work, they understand how far we still have to go in changing the mindset of venture capital.

"Successes are paramount," says Kerry, to begin to change the minds of those holding the purse strings. They are proud that all twelve companies in their first fund are still active, "healthy" and increasing in value. They recently raised a second, $30M True Wealth Ventures fund, with a thesis to invest in later stage companies with an enterprise focus (versus direct to consumer), that have de-risked their science or technology, and into which they can invest larger initial dollars. They have also recently published their first Impact Report with Impact Assets, a global effort to chart investments that are good for people and the planet. The report highlights the core metrics their companies are tracking to improve human health and/or the environment. These two women are paving the way for a new kind of venture firm, focused on doing well by doing good, all through a gender lens.

Anna Raptis: Amplifica Ventures

Listening to Anna talk of the challenges she faces raising her first gender lens fund in Mexico brings me back to ten years ago when we were starting JumpFund. The entrepreneurial ecosystem in Mexico and LATAM (Latin America) has been boosted in recent years by several powerful exits as well as the number of "unicorns" (companies valued at over $1B) increasing four fold in recent years. LATAM venture funds, predictably all-male-led, that are at their ten-year mark of maturity, are having great success, with companies like UBank, a Brazilian fintech, going public (IPO) in the U.S.

Yet, as a first-time, solo-female, gender lens fund manager, Anna has faced a tough road. Buoyed by the rise in women leading funds in the U.S., Anna set out to establish a fund that would address both the funding and capital gap for women in Mexico and LATAM more broadly. Australian by birth, Greek by heritage, Anna has spent much of her life abroad, including the Middle East, but has returned to Mexico where her husband has roots, excited to launch a female-focused fund. Her background in economic development, including with the United Nations, gave her a keen sense for both gendered economic disparities and the potential to increase women's economic participation in the world economy, both as investors and entrepreneurs.

In 2018, Anna attended her first Angel Capital Association conference in Boston, MA where she met like-minded women leading funds and networks supporting female founders. Having been quietly exploring the launch of her fund in Mexico, she felt like she had "come out of isolation" and saw another world open up to her. She has subsequently joined several U.S. based, women-led funds as a limited partner, primarily to watch and learn from them as she built her own. According to Anna, "you can't be what you can't see." Connecting with women in the trenches as angel investors, fund managers, and angel network leaders encouraged her to just go and do this herself. As an angel investor, she has followed the "learn by doing" model by jumping into deals as she is able and has taken a similar "build as you go" approach to her first fund, Amplifica Ventures.

Anna has seen forward progress in Mexico around angel investing, which is now seen as a more serious asset class with the potential for strong returns. Unfortunately, she feels LATAM is still way behind the U.S. in terms of addressing diversity and inclusion in business and specifically within early stage investing. The U.S. does not serve as much of a model, as our country is still grossly inequitable in many arenas for women and people of color as well.

"But what I do see in the U.S.," says Anna, "is that amongst a certain segment of the market, there's consciousness, and whether they're doing it because they want to increase their PR, or if they really believe it. I'm not 100% sure that really matters." Anna refers to the movement among American financial institutions and corporations to invest in underrepresented fund managers because they want to be part of publicly demonstrating their commitment that systemic change is needed. "A lot of work that I do is education," says Anna, "that you really can make money and drive returns, by investing in underrepresented fund managers and founders."

Her premise with Amplifica Ventures is to support and expand what others are doing, so she continues to engage as an active limited partner in seven other funds—5 in Mexico, 2 in U.S. and 2 in Australia—partly to share deal flow and also best practices. She is most interested in supporting other female general partners as she has had difficulty finding like-minded GPs in Mexico to join her own fund. Recruiting limited partners has also been a struggle, particularly among women who do not have a history in Mexican culture of being investors themselves. Similar to what JumpFund found with women investors in the Southeast U.S., many LATAM women tend to lean on third party advisors, whether that be their husbands, sons, or financial advisors, who do not necessarily see the need or opportunity of investing in a gender lens fund.

Mexico is currently 122nd out of 156 countries world-wide of women participating in its economy. The World Economic Forum has pronounced that if greater gender parity was achieved in many of these countries, their GDP (gross domestic product) could increase by as much as seventy percent. In fact, according to McKinsey research, gender equality could add up to $28 trillion to the world's economic output by 2050, in a scenario in which women play identical roles in labor markets to those of men. In countries ranked in the bottom 50% for gender equality, the gains are even more substantial - an increase in the size of the economy (GDP) by 35% on average.[30]

Anna's mission is to be a part of amplifying the need for gender parity across all aspects of the global economy. She references Melinda Gates in a recent article in The Conscious Investor whose research has found that it will take 208 years for the U.S. to reach gender equality, at the rate we are going.[31] "If that's in the U.S.," says Anna, "it's going to be a lot longer in Mexico and other countries in Latin America. So I can't not jump out of bed in the morning and work my hardest to make that change happen more quickly.

Arian Simone: Fearless Fund

"Most people who cut checks don't look like me," says Arian Simone, founding partner of Fearless Fund, an early stage venture fund in Atlanta, GA focused on access to capital for women of color. Arian and original co-founder, Keisha Knight Pulliam (who starred as Rudy Huxtable on *The Cosby Show*) started Fearless Fund in 2016 after a series of encounters at startup and venture capital events and conferences where they were the only Black women in the room. With an MBA and startup experience herself, running her own retail boutique and later a PR and marketing firm, Arian began to address this deficit in the market by building a network of thousands of followers through her Fearless community. Starting in 2010 with *Fearless* magazine, Arian grew the community adding events and pitch conferences featuring women of color at the headquarters of both Facebook in Silicon Valley and Spanx in Atlanta, GA.

When Arian was still a student at Florida A&M University, she raised a modest amount of capital to open her first retail boutique and found that she had little in common with most potential investors. "There was a promise that I made to myself when I was 21," recalls Arian. "I said, 'Don't you worry, because one day you'll be the business investor you were looking for.'" At the time, she had no idea that tiny seed would manifest into running her own venture fund, but she did know she wanted to be on the financial side of support for entrepreneurs that would have a return on investment.

As the Fearless community grew, Arian saw an opportunity to make good on her promise to herself to enter the world of venture capital and support other women. She admits that the "power of naivete" propelled her forward in the early days of establishing a fund as an emerging manager, with a goal of raising $5M and investing in many of the companies that had come through the Fearless network. JumpFund was an early investor in and mentor for her nascent fund, originally called the Women of Color Collective, as we saw an opportunity to grow our investments in BIPOC female founders and add more diversity to our portfolio.

After struggling to raise funds initially, Fearless Fund saw a boost with the racial reckoning in 2020 as more institutions became interested in supporting diversity and inclusion initiatives. To date, Fearless has now raised a total of $25.8M from Allied Bank, PayPal, Bank of America, JP Morgan and others. With less than 1% of venture capital funding going to people of color, there is a clear moral imperative for these large financial institutions to put their money where their mouth is. Arian says she benefited as a first-time fund manager from the guidance and connections people gave her early on. "Initially, it was not as easy as it is now for us, it was rough," says Arian, "but I was up for the challenge. I had no clue what I was really, truly getting myself into, but I have no regrets."

With investments now in over thirty companies led by women of color, many experiencing significant upward trajectories in growth in part due to the early support of Fearless Fund, Arian has clearly demonstrated that the pipeline of quality deal flow of BIPOC women-led companies is rich and investable. Several of the companies they've invested in have appeared on the cover of *Essence* and *Inc. magazines*. And the institutional investors with which they've engaged have remained active with their portfolio companies, providing C-suite mentoring and helping founders with access to education, social networks, and even additional funding.

Arian feels that part of the secret to their success was knowing what their "why" was from the beginning and surrounding themselves with supportive advisors and mentors as first-time fund managers. In the early days of starting Fearless Fund, Arian reached out to JumpFund and utilized our fund formation documents and even our legal counsel (cheaper than Atlanta price tags) to help them get off the ground. One challenge she's come to realize, like many first-time fund managers, is that even with a $25M fund, a 2% management fee does not adequately cover the real costs of running an early stage venture enterprise. Luckily for Fearless, they have been able to rely on grant support to bolster their ten person staff, which includes an investment analyst and fund administrators. The change Arian would ultimately like to see is that VC funds and angel investors would dedicate a minimum of 25-30% of their investment dollars to women and people of color. A lofty goal which Arian and the Fearless Fund has proven is more than possible.

Valerie Novacoff Britten: Broadway Women's Fund

Valerie Novacoff Britten sees closing the gap between the percentage of women in Broadway theater audiences (63%) and women in "C suite" decision-making roles in major productions as a clear business opportunity. Historically, less than 13% of Broadway shows are written or directed by women and only 25% of producers are female. Yet, women-led shows have been proven to outperform at the box office.

As we've mentioned before, the term "angel investor" originates from Broadway, where producers and investors back shows that are either huge successes with great returns or complete flops and total losses. Valerie, who understands both private equity and the world of Broadway, has seen the movement towards more gender parity in both markets and wanted to address the problem herself. Starting her career as a finance assistant for the show Wicked, where she helped run operations backstage, including human resources, payroll, and production fundraising. Through this experience and later roles as General Manager on other big shows, she witnessed a clear power dynamic in the industry, which was dominated by men.

Much as JumpFund wondered early in our fund's journey, Valerie constantly asked herself and others, "Where are the women?" She is often told by industry executives, "I would love to hire more women. I just don't know who is qualified, and I don't have the bandwidth to vet them."

Although there are a few other venture funds on Broadway, none were addressing the gender gap or using a gender lens to invest in shows, and none were certainly run by women. A fellow backstage bookkeeper challenged Valerie as to what they might do about the gender gap they were both seeing in their roles holding the purse strings and cutting checks. While the other woman has gone on to start a nonprofit addressing the pipeline of more women in lucrative, backstage and production roles, Valerie saw a chance to challenge the status quo and build a fund that would invest only in women-led shows, on the thesis that investing in women on Broadway is good business.

Valerie's ultimate goal is to see gender parity in leadership on Broadway. In the last full season before the pandemic, only 13% of shows were directed by women and the same number (13%) of shows were written by women. Women actually represent a larger number of producers, approximately 20-25%, but this is nowhere near equal to male producers. "I saw these venture and private equity funds starting to say that when you put women in positions of power and leadership roles, it's not just the right thing to do, it's a good business decision," says Valerie. Which led her to believe the same might be true on Broadway. Digging into the data she found that women-led shows outperform substantially, specifically musicals. "When there's more than one woman on the leadership team of a musical," says Valerie, "the financial recoupment rate is 55% while the industry standard is about 20 to 25%."

Valerie had the misfortune of launching her Broadway Women's Fund (BWF) in January 2020, and within three months all of Broadway was shut down by the pandemic. In a recent BWF update from Valerie, she shared data from the National Women's Law Center published in January 2022, that men have completely recouped pandemic employment losses, while 1.1 million fewer women are participating in the labor force than did in February 2020. Valerie states, "as Broadway begins to bounce back, we must make sure women make up for lost ground in order to achieve our goal of gender parity among leadership roles."

It's been more than three years of uncertainty in the theater industry, but Valerie has held onto the opportunity and impact her fund can make and raised more than half of her $2.5M first fund goal. With this small "proof point" fund, she will be able to invest in 5-10 shows with investment opportunities such as "Suffs," a musical about the Suffragette movement, which opened in the Spring of 2022 at the Public Theater. Similar to investing in startups, investors in a Broadway show generally write $25k-200k checks while producers invest $200k or more. If the show does well, all investors recoup their money, while 50% of any profits go to the producers as they underwrote a larger portion of the production and had more to lose.

In tandem with launching the Broadway Women's Fund, Valerie started an annual list called *Women to Watch on Broadway* which features mid-career women who are excelling in their fields but have yet to be considered leaders in the industry, proof that there is no "pipeline issue" of female leadership on Broadway. Since starting BWF, Valerie has had outreach from producers looking to put "women above the title" on a number of shows, so she knows she is already making an impact.

Although getting started has been doubly difficult for Valerie during the pandemic, given the full shutdown of the industry in which she had planned to invest, she still sees great potential for BWF. Her advice to anyone launching a new fund is to think BIG and don't limit yourself. After this first micro-fund, with which she intends to prove both her pipeline and profit model, Valerie intends to build a second $25-50M fund to elevate the role of women's leadership on Broadway. She has drawn inspiration from other industries, particularly private equity, which has seen a rising tide of gender lens investing. Her intention is to bring a gender lens to the very male-dominated world of entertainment—think Harvey Weinstein, Scott Rudin, and other powerful and abusive industry moguls.

Valerie also knows you must have resilience and determination as a first-time fund manager, and especially as a woman. As more stories of women doing this for themselves emerge, and women in positions of power are portrayed in the public eye, be it on television, on stage, or in real life, Valerie is seeing a shift in the conversation about women's leadership. According to Valerie, "This is about changing hearts and minds," which is a slow process, but one she is determined to help lead.

Marcia Dawood: The Angel Next Door

"Go beyond giving, invest in change" is Marcia Dawood's mantra. She wants more people, especially women, to understand the real opportunity and impact of angel investing. As an active investor in several women-led angel funds and networks, she is on a mission to help potential angel investors understand that total philanthropic giving in the U.S. represents only 1% of the overall valuation of the U.S. stock market. Through her podcast, *The Angel Next Door* and her TEDx talk, "Do Good While Doing Well," Marcia hopes to demystify angel investing, especially for women, and move more private capital to entrepreneurs. If more investors understood how they could pay it forward by investing in businesses they care about, whether that is with a gender lens or just those in their own backyard, the rewards would be manifold.

Marcia's journey into angel investing began in 2011 when she was invited to a gathering of the Blue Tree Angel Network, a Philadelphia-based angel group run by then Angel Capital Association Chair Catherine Mott. Marcia and her husband Izzy Dawood, a career CFO, were looking for alternative investment opportunities at the time and decided to join Blue Tree as active members. A few years later they moved to New York City and Marcia started looking for a local angel investment group and discovered Golden Seeds. As she learned more about Golden Seeds mission to increase access to capital for female founders and the data on the funding gap for women, she began focusing her angel investing on mainly women-led companies. "When I joined Golden Seeds, I had no idea how little capital went to women, and as soon as I found that out, I changed my entire investment thesis," says Marcia.

With a renewed purpose to invest in women, Marcia joined the first Rising Tide pilot fund with Alicia Robb, became an early investor with Portfolia (and later their COO), and then joined Next Wave Impact Fund as one of the nine members of its Investment Committee. Through her work with Next Wave, Marcia met Heather Henyon, an American angel investor living in Dubai, UAE who was running the Women's Angel Investor Network (WAIN), the first network in the Middle East (MENA) focused on female founders. Fast forward to 2018, Marcia jumped in to help Heather who was launching her own gender lens fund, Mindshift Capital, with an emphasis on cross-border investments given Heather's MENA connections. To date, they have raised a $7M fund and have invested in 17 companies, both in the U.S. and MENA region with a focus on FinTech, FoodTech, Health, and EdTech.

Marcia says the hardest part about launching a fund is

the fundraising. This is a pain point for many emerging fund managers, but especially for women. She sees the issue for Mindshift as twofold: 1) women investors get excited about the opportunity but then back off when it comes to actually investing, sometimes with the excuse that their husbands or financial advisors tell them it's not a good investment; 2) Mindshift's interest in cross-border investments has caused both U.S. and MENA investors to back away, as they are concerned about investing outside of their own country. Although Mindshift has de-risked this issue by housing the fund in the Cayman Islands and handling all of the complexities of international investing, they had pushback from potential investors that it is outside of their wheelhouse.

Working for over a decade to grow women's capital and impact in angel investing, including serving as Chair of the Angel Capital Association as well as a member of the SEC's Small Business Capital Formation Advisory Committee, Marcia has seen some common trends. Her advice to those looking to start a new fund or network is to start in one of two ways. Either creating smaller special purpose vehicles (SPVs) where investors can pool their money to invest in one company. Or start an "annual fund" such as the ones she helped structure at Blue Tree and Golden Seeds. An annual fund allows someone to be a member of a group but instead of investing in companies individually, they commit a sum one-time per year. Smaller investments, $25,0000 or less, are more palatable to female investors not used to writing large checks of $100,000-250,000—the expectation of most venture funds. Many platforms now exist that help provide back-office support and structure for emerging, smaller funds and SPVs, such as Loon Creek Capital, CARTA, or AngelList. These types of funds can also be structured for more of a "learning by doing" model where the limited partners all get a chance to vote on each investment, be a part of diligence teams, or choose to sit back and be passive members of a more diverse portfolio of investments than they would writing individual checks to entrepreneurs.

Of all the women-led companies she's invested in thus far, Marcia is excited about many but particularly proud of Cognition Therapeutics, working on a treatment for Alzheimer's, in which she invested early through Golden Seeds and went public (IPO) in 2021. She is also a fan of Joylux, a women's health company addressing vaginal health and pelvic floor issues at every stage of a woman's adult life. Marcia invested in the company through several different gender lens funds and as of 2023, Joylux has sold over 100,000 menopausal products and has over $12M in total sales.

If she could wave a magic wand and change something within the angel investing ecosystem, she'd like to alter people's view that angel investing is just for the ultra-rich. "The reality TV show *Shark Tank* has given people a false sense of angel investing, the perception that you have to be a billionaire or have a private plane," says Marcia. "I don't think people realize that this is an asset class that's accessible to all thanks to crowdfunding." She wants more people to understand that there's an entrepreneur in everyone's backyard and an angel investor potentially right next door.

These courageous, bold, innovative women leaders are a few of the many who are rising up and challenging the status quo of early stage, angel investing. Each has a slightly different thesis and mission, but all are dedicated to moving the needle on equity for female founders and engaging more women as agents of change through investing. I am proud to call them my friends and colleagues, and together we are growing women's capital to have more influence on the products, services, and company leadership growing our world economy. We are investing in the change we want to see in the world and hope others will see the opportunity to "do good by doing well."

Finding Your Joy

As I have watched other women establish gender lens investment funds and networks over the past 10 years, I have realized that we all find joy in this work. Beyond the potential for economic benefit, both for ourselves and the founders we invest in, there is a deep sense of meaning and purpose. What we are doing matters, and it is continually reinforcing to see the passion and activism emerge among women who are pooling their resources to invest in change.

In Karen Welborn's *The Lightmakers Manifesto: How to Work for Change without Losing Your Joy*, she speaks of the "whispers" activists often hear that ultimately lead them to take real action toward making a difference, with whatever cause they care deeply about. After over twenty years in education, I found myself listening to an inner voice calling out my radical feminist. The vast inequities I witnessed both among my female business students as well as female entrepreneurs writ large were appalling—what could I possibly do to help?

The whispers were becoming louder as I learned how to be an angel investor and saw the huge gaps in funding for women building businesses. My activist self was awakened and wanted to do more. By finding my tribe of like-minded women through launching JumpFund, joining forces with other women across the country in our Growing Women's Capital network, and my later work with Next Wave Impact, we have been able to harness our collective purpose to invest in women and change the game.

Out of this radical shift in my career and leaning into a deeper meaning and purpose in my life, I have found great joy in this work. Many angel investors, men and women alike, have found similar joyfulness in supporting other people's dreams and watching them come to fruition. I love coaching women who are just starting out, and trying to decide if and how they should raise capital. I am proud when any one of our companies reaches another major milestone, whether that's exceeding their revenue goals or raising more money for growth. And I am gleeful when an investment realizes a long-promised positive exit, especially knowing that we were one of their first investors and greatest cheerleaders.

Through this work, I have been able to put my deeply held beliefs about women's rights and equity into action with a like-minded group of women, spanning across the country. While we may come from widely different political views, we can all rally around the lack of adequate funding for female founders. Most of the other women I work with who run funds or networks are not in it to be career venture capitalists. But rather embrace a deeper mission of "doing it for ourselves" and proving that women can be both good investors and strong investments.

How can you make a difference in your own community using your passion and purpose, your talents and resources? What is whispering to you?

Final Act

The Ripple Effect

FINAL ACT

The Ripple Effect

When we invest in women and girls, we are investing in the people who invest in everyone else.

—Melinda Gates

As of the writing of this book, we have retreated further backwards in the overall percentage of venture funding going to female founded companies—currently hovering at 2% of venture capital, the lowest it's been since 2016. Yet, I am buoyed by the number of new funds and networks led by women and those investing with a gender lens. Fabric VC, Stella Impact Capital, and Zane Ventures are all newer funds focused on women (or women of color), and there are many more coming up alongside them. And, the exponential rise of women angel investors, from only 5% when we launched our first fund in 2013 to more than 30% of the total number of angel investors in the U.S. is cause for celebration.

At a recent in-person gathering of our Growing Women's Capital network at the ACA, it was heartening to reconnect with our partners in this movement. As Loretta McCarthy of Golden Seeds told the group, twenty years ago when their angel network was just getting started, people were shocked that there might even be women-led companies in which to invest and now they have funded more than 240 female founded companies across the U.S. with several very successful exits. Our movement of women investing in women today is more mature and sophisticated, with women having launched angel funds or networks 10-15 years ago and now considering how they might pay it forward to the next generation of emerging group leaders. Bright spots of women doing this for themselves continue to pop up all over the country, such as a recent group of women in Connecticut, the Tidal River Fund, led Galia Gichon, a Next Wave limited partner who was interested in forming a group in her own backyard to grow community with other women investors. Or the success of the tenth annual Women's Venture Summit in San Diego—led by Dr. Silvia Mah of Stella Labs, an angel investor and women's entrepreneurship champion—which drew a sold out crowd of over 400 women interested in investing in women.

Encouraging signs of progress also include the types of companies we are now seeing founded and funded by women for women. FemTech is a burgeoning industry, less than ten years old, that specifically addresses health and wellness issues related to women. Women-led early stage funds and networks, including Mindshift Capital, True Wealth Ventures, Portfolia, Next Wave and Jump-Fund, have been among the first investors in this space. Female funders see huge value and opportunity as we are the end consumers of products addressing menopause, maternal health, and women's sexual health and want to capitalize on innovation to make our lives better. In fact, a recent report cited that female founded companies are outperforming all-male teams on exit potential by thirty percent! And, according to Pitchbook, even in this difficult market, female founders had lower median burn rates, greater valuation growth at the early stage, and lower valuation declines at later stages compared to all-male founded companies year-over-year.[32]

With more women holding the purse strings, and bringing their own, gendered lens to early stage investing, we will begin to see real change for female founders. Women have more power, opportunity, and wealth than ever before. By 2025, women will inherit $28 Trillion and by 2030 women will control 66% of wealth in the U.S.. We must leverage that power and privilege to fund more women-owned businesses.[33] With women starting roughly half of all new businesses in the U.S. in 2022, yet still receiving less than two percent of startup capital, the time is now to activate women investors to invest in the companies we want to see in the world.

In addition to growing women as angel investors, there is a movement afoot to increase the number of women in venture capital overall. In June 2023 an organization called How Women Lead, a network of 20,000 female executives advocating for gender equity, rang the closing bell on Wall Street to launch their New Table campaign in response to the enormous gender gap that exists in venture capital. While the number of women angel investors has seen growth over the past several years, the number of women in later stage venture capital has stagnated at only 8 percent, which is reflected in the overall amount of venture capital invested in female founders. "Although women have more power and wealth than ever before, there is still a huge gap in venture capital funding," according to Julie Castro Abrams, founder and chief executive officer of How Women Lead, "our needs as women investors aren't being met and investments are not reflecting our values or interests."[34] The New Table campaign's goal is to bring 10,000 women into venture capital investing by 2024.

We have learned much in ten years since we launched our first fund, and I hope you found the stories from our team, other fund managers, or even our inspiring entrepreneurs useful as you pursue your own passion and ways to invest in the change you want to see in the world. For those looking to start an angel group or fund, I hope the basics I provided on set-up, terminology, and best practices will be helpful as you begin your learning journey in this new, exciting, and impactful space. Key learnings from JumpFund's experience as first-time, female, gender lens fund managers include:

→ **Investing in women-led ventures CAN produce strong returns** on investment, and may even present an "arbitrage" market opportunity as long as access to capital remains an issue (which unfortunately it will for a long time to come).

→ **There ARE women out there (like you!) who want to become angel investors** and make early stage company investments. Our numbers have grown to almost a ⅓ of all angel investors in the past ten years and new female fund managers are continuing to emerge across the U.S. and globally.

→ **Building your network of like-minded investors,** whether they be gender lens, impact, or regionally focused, is beneficial to expanding strong deal flow and creating even more access to capital for the companies in which you invest.

→ **Educate yourself** and your fellow investors, whether you are starting out on your own or in a group. Those new to angel investing, join an existing group and learn alongside others before you take off on your own.

→ **Tap into your social and professional circles** to find other women in your backyard interested in engaging in angel investing—you will be surprised at what you find!

→ **Pay it forward**, always, and remember that we will only grow stronger together.

Success stories are also going to be a key factor in turning the tide and leveling the playing field for female founders (and women in VC). Gender Lens Investing funds need to see big exits. More women need to be seen as leaders of unicorn-potential companies. And those female entrepreneurs need more multi-million dollar acquisitions or even IPOs to be able to pay it forward and build a stronger network of women investing in women. In the world of high stakes investments, the more wins and displays of strong performance leads to more checks and more open doors.

Whether you are an entrepreneur, a first-time angel investor, or someone looking to gather a tribe of like-minded investors and build your own angel network or fund, I hope you found inspiration and practical knowledge in this book. Women are "doing it for ourselves" because we have seen the untapped opportunity of investing in female founders and know first hand the bias, sexism, and uphill battle these women face. We encourage you to jump in, take that first leap, whether you are building or investing in a woman-led company. If we don't do it, the landscape of venture capital and entrepreneurship will continue to be "pale, male and stale" as longtime angel investor, friend and colleague Elaine Bolle, loves to say. We are dedicated to changing the narrative, one gender lens investment at a time so that in the not so distant future, **we can make ANYWHERE the best place for a woman to invest in or grow a business.**

Acknowledgments

First and foremost, I want to thank my JumpFund partners—Betsy, Cory, Kim, Shelley, Stefanie and Tiffanie—who jumped in to build this startup of our own and brought their own superpowers to making our dream work. And a huge debt of gratitude to the 100+ women (and a few good men) who saw the opportunity to invest in the change they wanted to see with the first women-led angel funds in the Southeast U.S.—you are the most courageous and badass of them all.

Thank you to my early mentors in angel investing, Loretta McCarthy and Barbara Raho at Golden Seeds and Chattanooga Renaissance Fund founders David Belitz and Charlie Brock. Thanks to my friends and colleagues at LaunchTN, the Company Lab and the Angel Capital Association who continue to help me and JumpFund expand our impact. Many thanks to my editor and publisher, Chad Prevost of Big Self Books, who put up with my eternal procrastination and multitude of revisions to birth this book. And to Heather Cabot, whose insightful, journalistic storytelling and early recognition of the JumpFund inspired me to share our story.

Ongoing gratitude for the angel investing sisterhood I am so privileged to be a part of as we work together to grow women's capital and impact: Marcia Dawood, Alicia Robb, Heather Henyon, Silvia Mah, Sue Baggott, Janine Firpo, Wingee Sin, Jodi Pederson, Galia Gichon, Dawn Batts, Anne Maghas, Elaine Bolle, Geri Stengel, Meredith Haviland, my Next Wave, Mindshift and Golden Seeds sisters, and so many others—thankfully the list keeps growing! Recognition also goes to the many women I continue to meet and cheer on as they start their own funds and networks or launch as angel investors—we need more of you to jump in! And to the women starting new ventures across this country, I applaud you and hope that your success will continue to have a positive impact on unlocking access to capital for all underserved entrepreneurs.

And a very special thank you to my family who has cheered me all along the way, from launching the first JumpFund to writing this book. My daughter, Chapin, who offered thoughtful edits; my husband Tom who reviewed many drafts and is always present with his love, admiration, and support; and my son Max, who inspires me to find passion and joy in all that I do. My mother, who has always been an inspiration in my work and life, and set an example as someone who works for the greater good and is a curious, lifelong learner. I honor the women who have come before me, generations fighting for our equality and freedoms. I will continue to carry the banner and fight for a future where one day, we will not have to question why women-led companies receive less than 3% of early stage capital or whether women's innovations are just as worthy of investment. Onward!

Notes

1. Robinson, Jessica. *Financial Feminism*. Unbound, 2021, pp. 216-217.

2. Tech founders who lived in their "cheeto-eating" friends' basements had become a local meme at that time from a video created by the LampPost Group about solo, isolated founders. https://vimeo.com/28522571

3. Cabot, Heather & Samantha Walravens. *Geek Girl Rising*. St. Martin's Press, 2017, p.87.

4. The Women's Entrepreneurship Initiative, City of Atlanta. https://www.weiatlanta.com

5. Biegel, Suzanne, et al. *Project Sage 4.0: Tracking Venture Capital, Private Equity, and Private Debt with a Gender Lens.* Wharton Social Impact Initiative and Catalyst at Large, December 2021. https://esg.wharton.upenn.edu/wp-content/uploads/2022/08/project-sage-4.0.pdf

6. Perry, Mark. "Women Earn Majority of Doctoral Degrees." American Enterprise Institute, 2020, www.aei.org/carpe-diem/women-earned-majority-of-doctoral-degrees-in-2019-for-11th-straight-year-and-outnumber-men-in-grad-school-141-to-100

7. Nobel, Carmen."Venture Investors Prefer Funding Handsome Men." *Harvard Business Week,* 2014, www.hbswk.hbs.edu/item/venture-investors-prefer-funding-handsome-men

8. Kanze, Diana, et al. "Male and Female Entrepreneurs Get Asked Different Questions by VCs." 2017, hbr.org/2017/06/

male-and-female-entrepreneurs-get-asked-different-questions-by-vcs-

9. First Round Capital. "10 Year Project." 2015, www.10years.firstround.com

10. Robinson, Jessica. *Financial Feminism.* P. 3-4.

11. Abeyta,Lisa. "Women Now Make Up Almost 5 Percent of Investors in U.S.." *Inc. 2020,* www.inc.com/lisa-abeyta/women-now-make-up-almost-five-percent-of-investors-in-us.html

12. Flynn, Colleen. "Part Two: TN Female Founder Ecosystem." Medium 2019, www.flynniie.medium.com/female-founders-d32faa5f7527

13. Brooks, Alison Wood, et al. "Investors prefer entrepreneurial ventures pitched by attractive men." *Proceedings of the National Academy of Sciences of the United States of America (PNAS),* March 10, 2014, https://www.pnas.org/doi/10.1073/pnas.1321202111

14. Benner, Katie. "Women in Tech Speak Frankly on Culture of Harassment." *New York Times,* June 30, 2017, https://www.nytimes.com/2017/06/30/technology/women-entrepreneurs-speak-out-sexual-harassment.html

15. Silverstein and Sayre, "The Female Economy," *Harvard Business Review,* 2009, www.hbr.org/2009/09/the-female-economy

16. West, Collin and Gopinath Sundaramurthy. "Women VCs Invest in Up to 2x More Female Founders." *Kauffman Fellows,* March 25,2020, www.kauffmanfellows.org/journal_posts/women-vcs-invest-in-up-to-2x-more-female-founders

17. Silversteinm, Michael J. and Kate Sayre. "The Female Economy." *Harvard Business Review,* September, 2009, https://

hbr.org/2009/09/the-female-economy

18. Gonzales, Matt, "Nearly 2 Million Fewer Women in Workforce," *SHRM* 2022, www.shrm.org/resourcesandtools/hr-topics/behavioral-competencies/global-and-cultural-effectiveness/pages/over-1-million-fewer-women-in-labor-force.aspx

19. Bittner, Ashley and Brigette Lau. "Women Led Startups Received Just 2.3% VC funding in 2020." *Harvard Business Review,* February 25,2021, www.hbr.org/2021/02/women-led-startups-received-just-2-3-of-vc-funding-in-2020

20. ThePLUG Staff, "Lessons from Village Capital's Inaugural VC Pathways Report on Supporting Diverse Founders." *ThePLUG,* October 21, 2021, https://tpinsights.com/lessons-from-village-capitals-inaugural-vc-pathways-report-on-supporting-diverse-founders/

21. Morris, JP. "Coupa Aquires Connxus Adding a Wealth of Supplier Diversity Capabilities." *Spend,* April 5, 2020, www.spendmatters.com/2020/05/04/coupa-acquires-connxus-adding-a-wealth-of-supplier-diversity-capabilities

22. Key terms have been highlighted in bold and further definitions can be found in the Glossary of Angel Investing Terms in the Appendix.

23. Hayes, Adam. "Accredited Investor Defined." *Investopedia,* 2023, www.investopedia.com/terms/a/accreditedinvestor.asp

24. Harbison, John. "Angel Returns Beat All Asset Classes but Pose Greater Risk." *Angel Capital Association,* May 25, 2023, https://www.angelcapitalassociation.org/blog/angel-returns-beat-classes/

25. Angel Capital Association. "Angel Box Basics: A Guide Toward Forming an Active, Vibrant and Successful Angel

Organization." https://www.angelcapitalassociation.org/angel-box/

26. Women's Business Enterprise National Council. "Everything you need to know about WBENC Certification for women-owned businesses." www.wbenc.org/certification

27. Ehlinger, Maija. "SuperFan Acquisition is a Big Win for Southeast Women Investors & Entrepreneurs." *Hypepotamus,* October 7, 2021, www.hypepotamus.com/startup-news/superfan-acquisition-kentucky

28. Glaner, Joanna, "Here are the New 2021 Unicorn Startups Founded by Women," Crunchbase News, www.news.crunchbase.com/news/here-are-the-new-2021-unicorn-startups-founded-by-

29. Desvaux, Georges, et al. "Women Matter: Ten Years of Insight on Gender Diversity." *Mckinsey,* October 4,2017, www.mckinsey.com/featured-insights/gender-equality/women-matter-ten-years-of-insights-on-gender-

30. Robinson, *Financial Feminism*, p. 215.

31. Unknown."Women in VC: Anna Raptis of Amplifica Capital." *The Conscious Investor,* June 24, 2021, www.theconscious-investor.co/blog/women-ventura-capital-anna-raptis-amplifica-capital

32. PR Newswire. "Pitchbook Report on Women in VC Ecosystem Highlights Resilience and Strong Performance of Female Founders Amid Market Headwinds." *Yahoo Finance,* November 3, 2022, https://finance.yahoo.com/news/pitchbook-report-women-vc-ecosystem

33. Baghai, Pooneh, et al. "Women as the Next Wave of Growth in U.S. Asset Management." *McKinsey and Company,* June 29, 2020, https://www.mckinsey.com/industries/

financial-services/our-insights/women-as-the-next-wave-of-growth-in-us-wealth-management

34. Leech, Marie. "Initiatives Goal to Bring 10,000 Women into VC Investing." *bizWomen,* June 15, 2023, https://www.bizjournals.com/bizwomen/news/latest-news/2023/06/initatives-goal-to-bring-10-000-women-into-vc-in.html

Glossary of
Angel Investing Terms

This glossary serves as a reference for many of the angel investing terms found in this book or those most early stage investors will encounter. Many have been highlighted in the section "A Woman's Guide to Angel Investing." Resources used for term definitions include the Security and Exchange Commission's online glossary *Cutting Through the Jargon from A to Z* as well as the Angel Capital Association's online *Glossary of Terms Related to Venture Capital and Other Private Equity or Debt Financing.*

Accelerator

An accelerator is an organization or program that supports entrepreneurs and early stage businesses seeking to scale and accelerate their growth. Similar to incubators, accelerators offer a range of resources, such as training, mentorship, advisory support, and networking opportunities, which may also include access to potential funding sources or even direct investment in the companies that go through their program.

Accredited Investor

An investor that qualifies as an "accredited investor" per SEC Rule 501 guidelines. For example, individuals may qualify by having (1) annual income exceeding either $200K (singly) or $300K (with spouse or spousal equivalent) in each of the two most recent years; (2) more than $1 million in net worth, excluding the primary residence (singly or with a spouse or spousal equivalent); or (3) certain financial professional credentials.

Angel Investor

Angel investors are generally high-net-worth individuals who invest their own money directly in emerging businesses, typically in early funding rounds. Most angel investors are accredited investors and many are current or former entrepreneurs themselves

Assets Under Management (AUM)

AUM is the total market value of the investments managed by a person or entity on behalf of investors.

Berkus Method (aka Scorecard Method)

Used to calculate an early stage company's valuation. The Berkus/Scorecard Method assigns a number value ($500k) to the 5 factors most commonly used as risk metrics in early stage investment: Sound Idea (basic value), Prototype (technology risk), Management Team (execution risk), Strategy (market risk), Product rollout/Sales (production risk). The number value is a maximum that can be "earned" to form a valuation, allowing for a pre-revenue valuation of up to $2 million (or a post-money value of up to $2.5 million). This method is often used with very early stage, pre-revenue companies and does not necessarily take into account regional market valuations, or other aspects which might influence company pricing pre-investment.

Equity

While "equity" can refer to multiple concepts in the world of investing, in the context of capital raising, "equity" typically refers to an ownership interest in a company.

Cap Table

A capitalization (or cap) table names the holders of a company's equity securities (such as common stock, preferred stock, and convertible notes and warrants) and includes other related information, such as class of securities, number of shares or units held, purchase price and date of purchase or disposition.

Capital Call

The act of collecting capital from investors by an investment fund. Funds committed by Limited Partners in an angel or venture capital fund are "called" on a percentage basis over the investment period of the fund as needed to invest in private equity opportunities.

Carry

The percentage of profits, after returning investors' initial capital, that the General Partner of a venture fund realizes for its management role should the fund be successful.

Common Stock

Common stock is a type of security that represents an ownership interest—or equity—in a company, generally held by founders and key employees. Holders of common stock have rights that typically include the right to vote to elect members to a company's board of directors and to vote on certain corporate actions (such as takeover bids), and may have rights to dividend payments based on the company's profits. Common shareholders generally rank lower in liquidation preference on the cap table than preferred shareholders (the investors).

Convertible Note

A convertible note is a loan made by an investor to a company that can be converted at the next priced round of investment into equity (ownership interest) or potentially liquidated if the company sells before conversion. Convertible notes are often used during early stage seed rounds because of challenges valuing a company early in its life cycle.

Crowdfunding

Crowdfunding refers to a financing method in which money is raised through an online platform or other socialized method, soliciting relatively small individual investments or contributions from a large number of people. A "Regulation" crowd-funding offering is a type of exempt offering that permits a business to offer and sell its securities to the investing public through crowdfunding.

Demo Day

A showcase of startup companies invited to pitch on a specified day, often associated with a business accelerator, incubator, or investor forum.

Dilution

Dilution occurs when a company issues new shares of stock, leaving the existing stockholders with a smaller percentage ownership interest in the company.

Diversification

Diversification is an investment strategy to reduce the impact of any single loss by allocating investments across multiple asset classes, categories, or companies. Investors in early stage companies often use portfolio diversification, whether through pooled investment vehicles or as individual angel investors.

Due Diligence

Prospective investors typically evaluate an investment opportunity by conducting a due diligence review of a startup venture's potential risk/reward profile. Due diligence (DD) may include an analysis and weighting of any of the following: market opportunity, founding team, intellectual property/technology analysis, business model, and any legal or financial disclosures. Investors may solicit information using a standardized due diligence checklist, request access to relevant information, and host meetings with management to ask questions.

Exit Strategy

A company's exit strategy is the method by which it achieves returns for its investors and common shareholders. Exit strategies can include an initial public offering (IPO), an acquisition of the portfolio company, or a management buyout. These strategies depend on the exit climate, including market conditions and industry trends. An investment fund's exit strategy is the method by which it can liquidate its holdings (individual company investments) to achieve the maximum possible returns for its investors.

Funding Round

A funding round is when a company raises money from investors on the same or similar terms within a specific period. Rounds are often referred to by stage, starting with a *seed round,* followed by Series A and successively lettered Series rounds. A company's *valuation* generally increases with each successive funding round, and the purchase price per share increases accordingly.

General Partner

A general partner is an individual or an entity—typically affiliated with a venture capital firm, private equity firm, or other investment firm—that raises money from limited partners (investors) for a private fund organized as a limited partnership and that both invests in and manages the fund. A fund that is organized in a different structure, such as a limited liability company, has a managing member or other manager under applicable state law and governing documents of the fund instead of a general partner.

Incubator

An incubator is an organization that supports entrepreneurs and early stage companies, typically those that are still working to develop their business model and product or idea. Incubators can offer a range of resources, including training, advisory support, administrative support, mentorship, and networking opportunities or connections to investors and/or potential clients. Incubators often work with business ventures over a longer period than accelerators and some may provide funding or acquire equity in the business in exchange for their support.

Investment Thesis

The stated goal or focus of an individual investor, network, or fund regarding the purpose, type, size, and strategy of their investments. An investment thesis might include a focus on a particular industry, stage of investment, economic region, or "lens" such as social/environmental impact or gender. An investment thesis may also be related to the particular financial outcome anticipated for investments, such as targeted return profiles or annualized projected income.

Limited Partner

A limited partner is an investor who commits capital to a private fund. Unlike a general partner, a limited partner's participation in the fund's investment activities is restricted, and its liability for fund debt is limited to the amount of money that the limited partner contributed or committed to contribute. The relationship of a limited partner with the fund and the general partner is governed by a Limited Partnership Agreement. For a fund that is organized as a limited liability company, the investor is referred to as a member under applicable state law and governing documents of the fund.

Liquidation Preference

A liquidation preference is a right that an investor may have to be paid before other investors upon a liquidation event, such as the sale of the company. Preferred stockholders typically receive a liquidation preference over common stockholders. Liquidation preferences are often expressed as a multiple of the initial investment, such as 1X or 2X, plus accrued but unpaid dividends. Liquidation preference may vary by class of stock and may be negotiated during each funding round.

Management Fees

Management fees are fees generally paid out of fund assets to its advisor or general partner in exchange for managing the fund. For example, a private equity fund manager typically charges a fee based on a percentage of capital invested in the fund or committed to the fund, in addition to a performance fee. Management fees vary by fund type and structure, but a standard annual management fee is 1-3% of current assets under management.

Preferred stock/equity

Preferred stock is a type of security that represents an ownership interest or equity in a company with preferential rights over common stockholders. Preferred equity rights often include: liquidation preference, anti-dilution protection (such as pro-rata rights to invest in future funding rounds), dividend rights, and limited voting rights. In exchange for these rights, preferred stock is usually sold at a premium to the price of common stock, based on the company's valuation at the time of sale.

Managing Partner

A person who oversees the management and activities of a venture capital fund, often a member of the fund's general partner.

Option Pool

The number of shares set aside for the future issuance to employees of a private company.

Pitch competition

Similar to a Demo Day (see above), a pitch competition is an event at which startup companies present their business, generally with an associated "pitch deck," with a chance to win prize money and/or investment from participating investors or event sponsors.

Pre-Money Value

The valuation of a company prior to a round of investment. This amount is determined by using various calculation models. Later stage companies can be valued with venture capital methods such as discounted P/E ratios multiplied by periodic earnings or a multiple times a future cash flow discounted to a present cash value and a comparative analysis to comparable public and private companies. Earlier stage, pre-revenue companies often rely on "qualitative" measures such as an assessment of the founding team, market opportunity, value of intellectual property, competitive analysis, etc., or market comparison with companies in similar industries and regions of the country.

Pro rata rights

Pro rata rights are privileges granted to existing investors, usually owners of preferred equity, allowing them to retain their initial ownership percentage by participating in future financing rounds, thus maintaining their stake in the company.

Portfolio Company

Companies in which a given fund, group of investors, or individual has invested. A fund, group or individual angel or venture capital investor generally invests in a "portfolio" of companies over time.

Post-Money Value

The pre-money valuation on which share pricing is determined plus the total invested on that given valuation in any given round of fundraising. The post-money valuation then becomes the marker of current carrying value for company investors. For instance, if a pre-money value was set at $5M and $1M was invested in a particular funding round, the company would be valued at $6M post-money.

ROI (Return on Investment)

ROI measures the amount of return on a particular investment, relative to the investment's cost. To calculate ROI, the benefit (or return) of an investment is divided by the cost of the investment. The result is expressed as a percentage or a ratio.

Seed Round

A seed round is typically a company's first funding round, often raised from friends and family, angel investors, or early stage funds in exchange for a convertible note. Capital at this stage may be used for product development, market research, or early revenue traction.

Series A, B, C, + Rounds

After a Seed or initial round of equity financing, a company raises money on subsequent rounds often lettered according to increased valuation and size of total investment at each stage. For instance, a Seed round may be based on an initial company valuation of $5M and raise $1M in equity financing, while a Series A will be based on a company's relative progress towards agreed upon metrics (revenue, clients, technology, IP, etc) and priced at a higher valuation (eg. $15-20M with a $5M+ capital raise). Companies that raise Series B and later rounds are more mature companies that often have larger venture capital or institutional investors leading the financing. Angel investors typically invest in Seed and Series A rounds but may follow on in later rounds to avoid dilution.

Simple Agreement for Future Equity (SAFE)

A simple agreement for future equity (SAFE) is an agreement between a company and an investor in which the company promises to give the investor a future ownership interest in the company if certain triggering events occur, such as future equity financing or acquisition of the company. The owner of the SAFE does not have an ownership interest in the company unless the triggering event occurs and converts the instrument into equity. Like convertible notes, SAFEs are often used during seed rounds; however, unlike convertible notes, SAFEs generally do not include a valuation of the equity at the time of issuance, instead deferring that calculation until the triggering event occurs.

Stock

A stock is a security that represents an ownership interest—or equity—in a corporation. Equity holders of stock are often called "stockholders" or "shareholders." Different classes of stock, such as common stock and preferred stock, have different voting and economic rights. A stockholder's ownership interest is often reflected as either a percentage of stock or number of shares on the company's capitalization table.

Term Sheet

A summary of the terms an investor is prepared to accept. A term sheet is a non-binding outline of the principal points that the Stock Purchase Agreement and related agreements will cover in detail. These points generally include: company valuation, total capital raise, basic investor rights and preferences, as well as board composition and voting rights.

Valuation

A company's valuation, the worth of a company determined by an analyst or as agreed upon by the company and its investors, typically establishes how much the company and its investors value the company. The valuation establishes how much equity the investor will receive in exchange for its investment. See Pre-Money and Post-Money valuation definitions.

Valuation Cap

A valuation cap is used in a convertible note to give the note-holders a "ceiling" value at which their investment will convert. A convertible note also usually has a "discount" on conversion into future equity and the investor will convert on the greater of either the discount or the valuation cap relative to the pricing of the new equity round.

Vesting

Vesting is a mechanism where founders or employees earn ownership of their shares in a company over a period of time. The breakdown of this time period is referred to as a vesting schedule and its purpose is to both reward and retain employees within a startup company.

Recommended Reads

Books to inspire the angel investor in you.

The Startup Investor Mindset, Dr. Silvia Mah (2023)

Financial Feminism: A Woman's Guide to Investing for a Sustainable Future, Jessica Robinson (2021)

Geek Girl Rising: Inside the Sisterhood Shaking Up Tech, Heather Cabot and Samantha Walravens (2017)

Sexism in America: Alive, Well, and Ruining Our Future, Barbara J. Berg, Ph.D (2009)

Impact with Wings: Stories to Inspire and Mobilize Women Angel Investors and Entrepreneurs, Suzanne Andrews, Jagruti Bhikha, Karen Bairley Kruger, Christine Emilie Lim, Wingee Sin, and Hana Yang (2016)

The Lightmaker's Manifesto: How to Work for Change Without Losing Your Joy, Karen Walrond (2021)

All In: How Women Entrepreneurs Can Think Bigger, Build Sustainable Businesses, and Change the World, Stephanie Breedlove (2017)

Real Impact: The New Economics of Social Change, Morgan Simon (2017)

Level Up: Rise Above the Hidden Forces Holding Your Business Back, Stacey Abrams and Lara Hodgson with Heather Cabot (2022)

The Next Wave: Financing Women's Growth Oriented Firms,

Susan Coleman and Alicia Robb (2016)

Activate Your Money: Invest to Grow Your Wealth and Build a Better World, Janine Firpo (2021)

The XX Edge: Unlocking Higher Returns and Lower Risk, Patience Marime-Ball and Ruth Shaber, M.D. (2022)

Do Good While Doing Well: Invest for Change, Reap Financial Rewards and Increase Your Happiness , Marcia Dawood (2024)

About the Author

Kristina Montague is the managing partner of the JumpFund, an angel fund dedicated to engaging women's capital to invest in women-led companies across the Southeast U.S. She is also a partner in Next Wave Impact Fund and Mindshift Capital and since 2013 has built a portfolio of investments in female founded ventures. Following a 25+ year career in education, most recently as an Assistant Dean at University of Tennessee Chattanooga's Rollins College of Business, Kristina jumped into angel investing full time and serves on the board of the Angel Capital Association. She lives between Chattanooga, TN and Seattle, WA with her husband and is the proud mother of two grown children.